100 WALKS IN
Suffolk

compiled by

ROBERT H STONER

The Crowood Press

First published in 1996 by
The Crowood Press Ltd
Ramsbury
Marlborough
Wiltshire SN8 2HR

British Library Cataloguing-in-Publication Data
A catalogue record for this book is
available from the British Library

ISBN 1 85223 949 2

All maps by Janet Powell

Typeset by Carreg Limited, Ross-on-Wye, Herefordshire

Printed by Redwood Books, Trowbridge, Wiltshire

CONTENTS

35.	Boyton	4m	(6^1/$_2$km)
36.	… and longer version	8m	(13km)
37.	Needham Market & Priestley Wood	4^1/$_2$m	(7km)
38.	Lavenham	4^1/$_2$m	(7km)
39.	Cratfield	4^1/$_2$m	(7km)
40.	Pakenham	4^1/$_2$m	(7km)
41.	Great Ashfield	4^1/$_2$m	(7km)
42.	Halesworth	4^1/$_2$m	(7km)
43.	Claydon	4^1/$_2$m	(7km)
44.	Hintlesham	4^1/$_2$m	(7km)
45.	Great Glemham	4^1/$_2$m	(7km)
46.	Rendham	4^1/$_2$m	(7km)
47.	Earl Soham	4^1/$_2$m	(7km)
48.	Westhall	4^1/$_2$m	(7km)
49.	Lakenheath	4^1/$_2$m	(7km)
50.	Saxmundham	4^1/$_2$m	(7km)
51.	Kersey	4^1/$_2$m	(7km)
52.	Hawkedon	4^1/$_2$m	(7km)
53.	Brandeston	4^3/$_4$m	(7^1/$_2$km)
54.	Orford Castle and the River Ore	5m	(8km)
55.	Thorpeness and Sizewell	5m	(8km)
56.	Trimley Marsh and the River Orwell	5m	(8km)
57.	Walberswick and Tinkers Marsh	5m	(8km)
58.	Dedham and Flatford Mill	5m	(8km)
59.	Stutton and the River Stour	5m	(8km)
60.	Belstead	5m	(8km)
61.	Chelmondiston and Pin Mill	5m	(8km)
62.	Ixworth and the Two Mills	5m	(8km)
63.	Redgrave and Lopham Fens	5m	(8km)
64.	Blythburgh	5m	(8km)
65.	Hartest	5m	(8km)
66.	Santon Downham	5m	(8km)
67.	Stanton	5m	(8km)
68.	Bungay	5m	(8km)
69.	… and longer version	10m	(16km)
70.	Brandon	5^1/$_4$m	(8^1/$_2$km)

Publisher's Note

We very much hope that you enjoy the routes presented in this book, which has been compiled with the aim of allowing you to explore the area in the best possible way - on foot.

We strongly recommend that you take the relevant map for the area, and for this reason we list the appropriate Ordnance Survey maps for each route. Whilst the details and descriptions given for each walk were accurate at time of writing, the countryside is constantly changing, and a map will be essential if, for any reason, you are unable to follow the given route. It is good practice to carry a map and use it so that you are always aware of your exact location.

We cannot be held responsible if some of the details in the route descriptions are found to be inaccurate, but should be grateful if walkers would advise us of any major alterations. Please note that whenever you are walking in the countryside you are on somebody else's land, and we must stress that you should *always* keep to established rights of way, and *never* cross fences, hedges or other boundaries unless there is a clear crossing point.

Remember the country code:

Enjoy the country and respect its life and work
Guard against all risk of fire
Fasten all gates
Keep dogs under close control
Keep to public footpaths across all farmland
Use gates and stiles to cross field boundaries
Leave all livestock, machinery and crops alone
Take your litter home
Help to keep all water clean
Protect wildlife, plants and trees
Make no unnecessary noise

The walks are listed by length - from approximately 3 to 10 miles - but the amount of time taken will depend on the fitness of the walkers and the time spent exploring any points of interest along the way. All the walks are circular and most offer recommendations for refreshments.

Good walking.

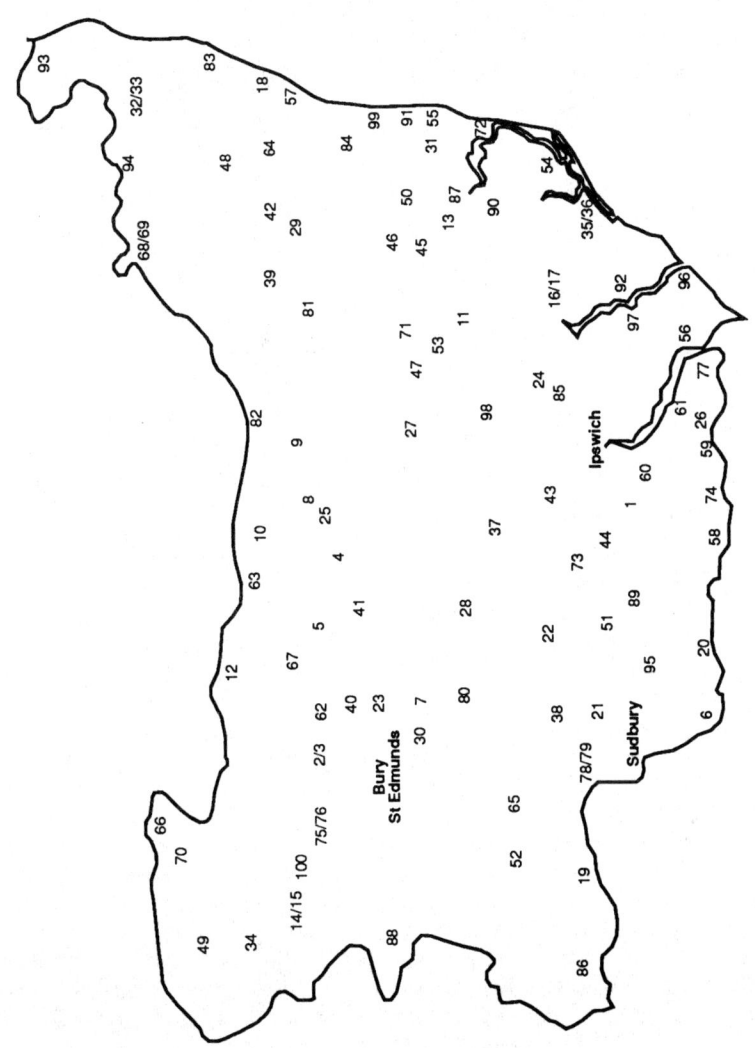

Walk 1   WASHBROOK AND COPDOCK   3m (5km)

Maps: OS Sheets Landranger 169; Pathfinder 1030.

A short walk, passing the parish churches.

Start: At 118421, the Brook Inn, Washbrook.

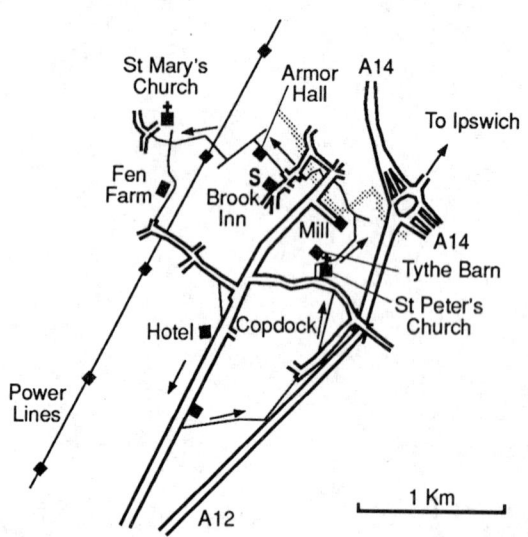

Walk down The Street and turn left along the driveway to Armor Hall, which used to be the Manor House of Washbrook. Pass the Hall, go through a gate and over a stile to join a main trackway. Turn left and follow the track uphill to reach a large tree and a junction of tracks. Turn right and follow the track to a stile. Cross the stile into a pasture and immediately turn left to follow the top edge of the field. Just before the corner of the field, either turn right and head downhill to visit the old, and now disused, parish church of **St Mary's**, or turn left over a stile to continue the route.

Follow the right-hand edge of the field to reach a track leading to farm buildings on your right. Turn right and follow the track to Hollow Lane. Turn left and follow the lane to a road junction. Continue straight on and, just after a bungalow on the right, turn right along a waymarked path. Follow the path across an arable field to reach the old A12 trunk road just behind the Copdock Hotel.

Turn right along the old road, then, just by Glebe Farm, turn left along a waymarked path. Follow the path through a paddock and down to the new main A12 trunk road, reaching it at its junction with an ancient trackway called Honey Lane. Turn left along Honey Lane (a green lane), passing a house on the left and continuing to reach a metalled lane. Maintain direction along this, but after some 150 yards, take a path on the left, going over a stile and down to reach another lane. Turn left and follow the lane to **St Peter's Church.**

Turn right just past the church – there is a 16th-century tithe barn on your left – and then right again to follow a path down to Copdock Mill. Go to the back of the mill, cross the Belstead Brook and then walk up to the old main road. Just before the road, turn left and follow a path under the road to reach Belstead Brook again. Now follow the path along the right-hand side of the brook, soon crossing to reach a recreation ground on the other side. Bear right and follow the track (Mill Lane) out to The Street. Turn left along The Street to return to the Brook Inn.

POINTS OF INTEREST:

St Mary's Church, Washbrook – Once the parish church of Washbrook, this church, dating from the 10th century, is now redundant.
St Peter's Church, Copdock – This is now the parish church of Washbrook and Copdock.

REFRESHMENTS:

The Brook Inn, Washbrook.
Washbrook village shop is also a useful source of refreshment.

GREAT LIVERMERE 3m (5km)
or 6m ($9\frac{1}{2}$km)

Maps: OS Sheets Landranger 155; Pathfinder 963.
A circular walk "across" Ampton Water.
Start: At 886713, in front of the lodge gates to Ampton Park in
Great Livermere.

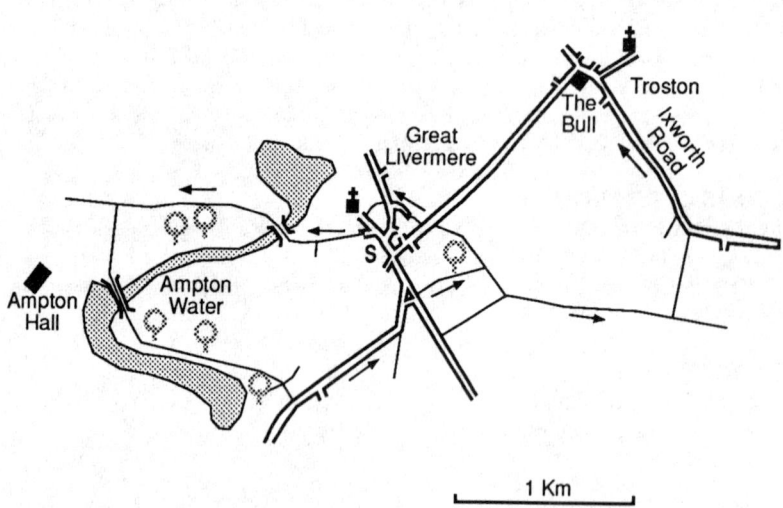

From the lodge gates, go along the driveway towards Ampton Hall. Soon you will
cross a bridge over the end of Ampton Water: continue along the driveway, with
arable fields to both the left and right until you reach a waymarked path on your left.
(The path is about 900 yards from the bridge.) Turn left along the path, crossing an
arable field and heading for a bridge to the left of the woods. Cross the bridge, over
Ampton Water, taking great care on this somewhat precarious looking structure. From
the bridge, on your right, there is a fine view of Ampton Hall. On the far side of the
water continue in the same direction, now going through woodland. After about
1,000 yards you will come out of the woods and on to a track: carry straight on,

crossing another bridge and then bearing slightly left to aim for a waymarker at the side of the field, next to the road. Turn left and follow the road to a junction.

To follow the shorter walk, bear left at the junction and then left again to return to the lodge gates and the walk's start.

The longer walk bears right just before the junction, following a short track to the road. Continue along the track opposite, soon reaching woodland. Pass to the right of the woods to reach the remains of a stile. Turn right and cross a field, reaching a track on the other side. Turn left and follow this track for a little over $^3/_4$ mile to reach a bridge on the left. Turn left and follow the path to a metalled road (Ixworth Road). Turn left and follow the road into the village of Troston, passing **Troston Hall** on your right. Turn right at the Bull and follow a lane towards Great Livermere. Just before some houses on the right, take a path, also on the right, and then bear left into a recreation ground. Follow the ground's right-hand edge and continue along a track to reach a metalled road. Turn right and, after a few yards, turn left along a path, with a flint wall on the right. At the end of the path, turn left in front of St Peter's Church and follow the lane back to the start of the walk.

POINTS OF INTEREST:
Troston Hall – The Hall was built in the 17th century for the Bacon family, relatives of Francis Bacon. In the 18th century the estate and Hall passed to the Lofft family of which Robert Lofft was a great benefactor to Troston. He restored the 13th-century St Mary's Church and also built the school and school house for the village.

REFRESHMENTS:
The Bull, Troston.

Walk 4   FINNINGHAM $3^1/_2$m ($5^1/_2$km)

Maps: OS Sheets Landranger 155; Pathfinder 985.

A circular walk along green lanes and across meadows.

Start: At 065691, the car park beside the White Horse, Finningham.

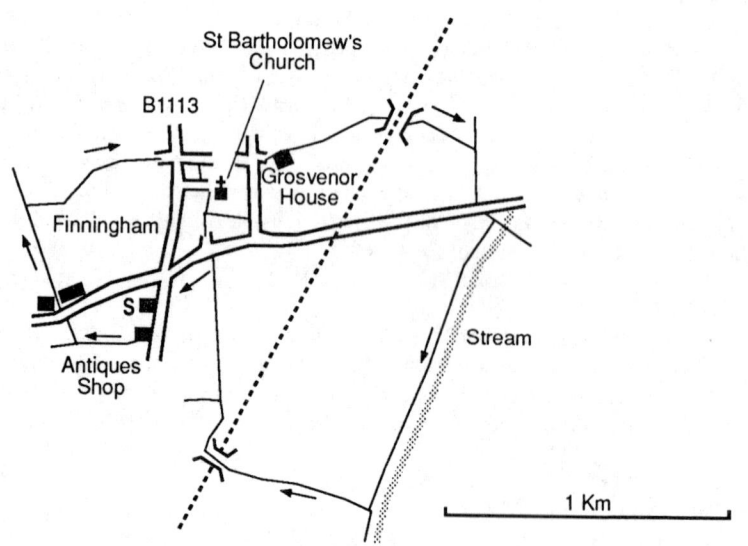

From the car park, turn right and follow the road to reach a small antiques shop, on the right. Turn right just beyond the shop to follow a track, passing a cottage on the left. Just before you reach a fence on the right, turn right to cross an arable field, heading towards a gabled cottage. This path might not be marked in a crop, but goes to the right-hand side of an electricity pole.

At the far side of the field, drop down on to a lane and turn left. After a few paces, turn right between bungalows, going along a green track. This track soon reaches an open field: follow the track along the right-hand side eventually coming to a T-junction of tracks. Turn right and walk along the top side of a meadow, heading towards a metal gate. Go through the gate and follow the track beyond to the main road (the B1113), reaching it opposite a T-junction. Cross the road, with care, and go along Gislingham Road. After a few paces, take the waymarked bridleway on your right, soon reaching a metalled lane. Cross and follow the path opposite to St Bartholomew's Church.

Just beyond the church, turn left to pass the main entrance, and then walk to the right-hand corner of the church from where the path continues to a metalled lane. Turn left along the lane and, just after crossing a small stream, turn right along a bridleway towards Grosvenor House. Just before the entrance to the house, bear left and follow the green lane towards the railway. Go under the railway and continue along the green lane to reach its T-junction with another track. Turn right, soon reaching a road.

Cross the road and follow the bridleway opposite, a grassy track with hedgerows on either side. The track soon opens out into a meadow: follow the path along the left-hand edge. Ignore a gap on the left, continuing along the left-hand side of the field, with a stream on your left. Continue into a second meadow and then walk through scrub to reach an arable field. Keep following the stream, with it on your left, passing a remnant hedge on your right to reach the next field. At the end of this small field, turn right along a waymarked bridleway, walking along the left-hand side of the field, with a hedgerow on your left. At the top of the field the path goes right, then left following a pleasant green track past a house on the right. The track soon comes to a T-junction: turn right and follow a gravel track over a railway bridge. Continue along the track to reach an electricity pole on your left. Turn right here to follow a waymarked path across an arable field heading towards **St Bartholomew's Church** in the distance. Follow the path to reach the main road in Finningham. Turn left and follow the road past the Old Post Office, on your left, to reach a crossroads by the White Horse.

POINTS OF INTEREST:

St Bartholomew's Church – The church is, in part, early 14th-century and has an ornate south porch. It is normally locked but the keys can be obtained – see note by main door.

REFRESHMENTS:

The White Horse, Finningham, at the start/end of the walk.

Walk 5 **WALSHAM LE WILLOWS** $3^1/_2$m ($5^1/_2$km)

Maps: OS Sheets Landranger 144; Pathfinder 963 and 964.

A walk through ancient woodland and a wartime airfield.

Start: At 999711, The Causeway, opposite the church in Walsham Le Willows.

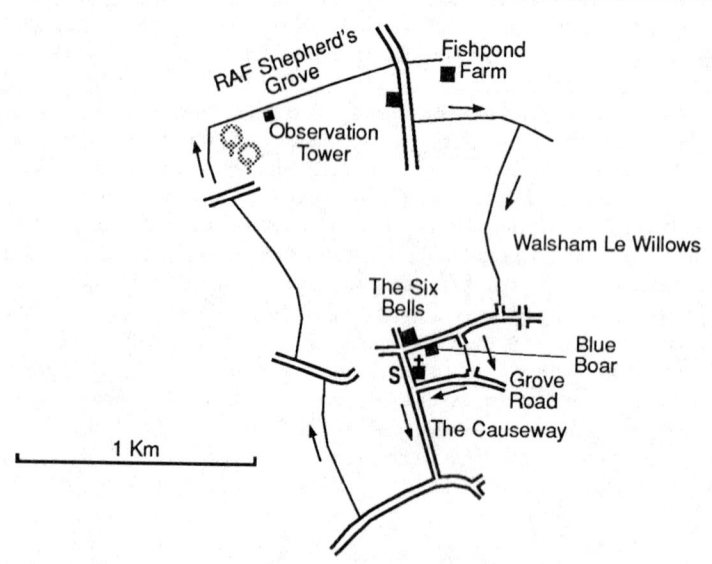

From the church, turn left to go downhill, passing a house called the Priory Room on your left. Follow the pavement down the left-hand side of the road, going over a bridge and past Grove Road, on your left, to reach a road junction. Continue along the main road, bearing right and passing Hill Cottage Nursery. After a further 300 yards, take a footpath on your right into a large open field. Follow the right-hand edge of the field to reach a metalled lane. Cross the lane and stile opposite, then turn left and follow a path with a stream, on your right, and a hedgerow and the lane on your left.

Soon you come to another stile: cross and turn immediately right over a bridge and stile into an open field. Cross another small stile and follow the right-hand edge of the field, with a hedgerow on your right and a small fence on the left. Go past a pond and then bear slightly left to come out into another open field. Follow the right-

14

hand edge of this field until you come to a concrete driveway. Cross the driveway and take the path opposite into woodland. The path takes you along the left-hand edge of the woods: where it opens out into a field, turn sharp right and re-enter the woods. Follow the path around the perimeter of the woods, coming out opposite a World War II observation tower on the disused **Shepherd's Grove Airfield**.

Keep straight on, with the tower on your right, following the green track. Soon the hedgerow on the left disappears: follow the right-hand side of a large field to reach a wooden gate and metalled road. Turn right and follow the road for some 200 yards, passing a new house on the right, to reach a waymarked track on the left. Follow this track for 500 yards to reach a track on your right, opposite a dead tree. Turn right and follow this track past a pond, on your left, and then open fields to both your left and right. After some 500 yards the path turns left, and then right, to go between houses and out on to the main road in Walsham Le Willows.

Cross the road, with care. Go over a stream and turn right to follow a tarmaced path in front of some houses. Just past 'Sideways Garage', on the right, turn left down a track, following it down to Grove Road. Turn right and follow the road to the junction with The Causeway. Turn right to return to the church.

POINTS OF INTEREST:
RAF Shepherd's Grove – This airfield was built in 1944 for the USAAF, but was used by RAF Bomber Command and then by RAF Transport Command. From 1951, the base was used by the USAF until the early 1970s when it finally closed.

REFRESHMENTS:
None actually on the route, but available at:
The Blue Boar, Walsham Le Willows.
The Six Bells, Walsham Le Willows.
The Post Office Stores in Walsham Le Willows is also a useful source.

Walk 6   **BURES AND ARGER FEN** $3^1/_2$m ($5^1/_2$km)

Maps: OS Sheets Landranger 155 and 168; Pathfinder 1052.

A walk through woods and meadows.

Start: At 908339, the car park in Nayland Road, Bures.

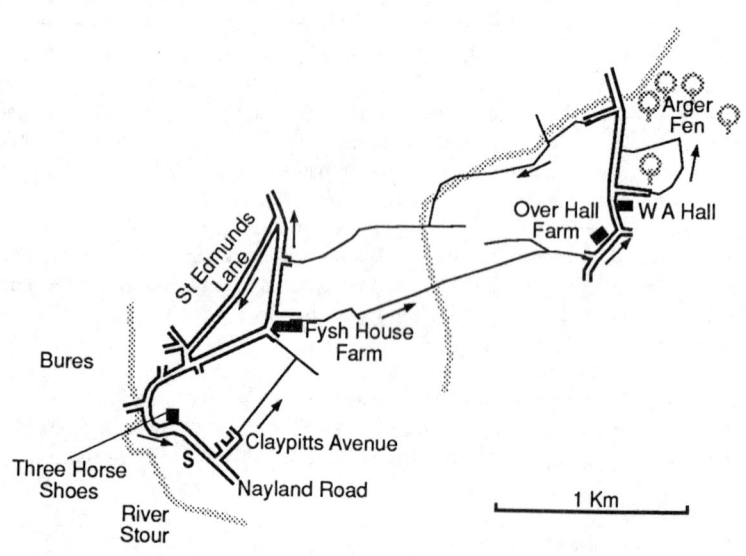

From the car park, turn right into Nayland Road and follow it past a primary school. Take the first turning on the left (Claypitts Avenue) and follow it for some 100 yards, ignoring a turning on the left. Where the road bears left, keep straight on, going uphill to pass to the right of a small wood. When you reach a concrete driveway, turn left along a track, passing in front of Cuckoo House. Continue along the track to reach a metalled road. Turn right along the road and, within a few yards, turn right again into Fysh House Farm. Follow the track, with a barn on your right, and, where it bears to the right, keep straight on along another track along the right-hand side of an arable field. Over to the left you can see the Sudbury TV Transmitter.

Follow the track downhill, then, where the track turns sharp right, keep straight on along a waymarked path, crossing arable fields to a stile and stream. Cross the stile and continue along the path over the stream. Go across a meadow, cross another stile

16

and keep straight on across another very large field, now heading to the right of farm buildings seen in the distance, (Over Hall Farm). At the far side of the field you will join a bridleway coming in from the left: continue along the bridleway with hedgerow on either side to reach a metalled lane.

Turn left, passing Over Hall Farm and continue along the road to reach W A Hall (Seed Merchants) on the right. Just past the main entrance, take the footpath on the right, following it to reach a metal gate and open field. Go into the field and follow its left-hand edge, keeping a wood (Arger Fen) on your left. When you reach the corner of the field, keep straight on, now going into the woods. Follow a wide track downhill to reach a junction of tracks. Turn left and follow the now waymarked track through the woods to reach a metalled lane just past a picnic site.

Turn right down the lane, but just before you reach a bridge over a stream, turn left along a path, with a house on your left. Now, just before you come to a building on your right, cross a stile also on your right and follow the path beyond to the back of the building. Continue along the path, with the stream on your right. Soon the path goes crosses a sleeper bridge: continue along the path with the stream now on your left. Just after you pass an artificial lake, on your right, the path crosses the stream again: continue along the path with the stream now on your right again.

Follow the path to its junction with a track and turn right to follow the track past Moat Farm, on your right. Continue to reach a metalled road. Turn right and then, after some 250 yards, turn left to go down St Edmund's Lane. Follow the lane down into **Bures**. Turn left at a road junction and then bear right into the High Street. At the end of the High Street, bear left into Nayland Road (with the church on your right) and follow the road back to the car park.

POINTS OF INTEREST:
Bures – At the end of the 19th century Bures was a thriving town firstly with busy canal traffic and then (from 1850) with railway traffic. Nowadays trade is in decline and Bures is becoming more of a dormitory town.

REFRESHMENTS:
The Three Horse Shoes, Bures.
The Post Office and the Central Stores in Church Square are also useful sources.

Walk 7   **BEYTON** $3^1/_2$m ($5^1/_2$km)

Maps: OS Sheets Landranger 155; Pathfinder 984.

A walk around the village, passing the Norman Church.

Start: At 933632, the car park next to the White Horse, Beyton.

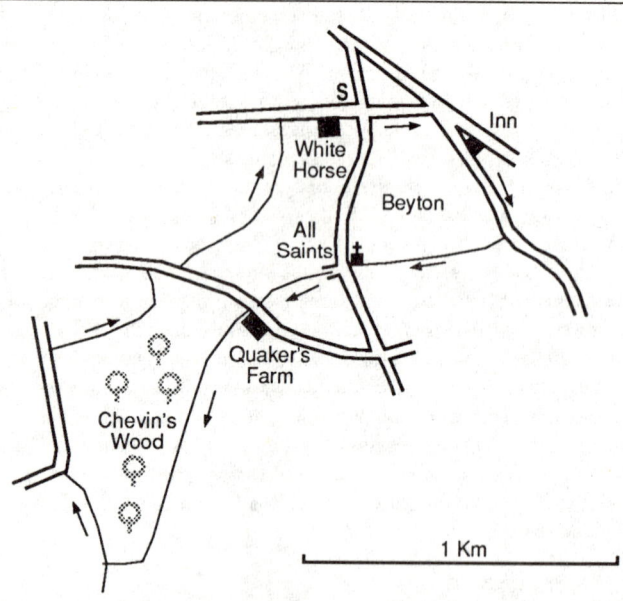

From the car park, turn right along the main road, passing the village green on the left. At the end of the green, turn right down the lane signposted to Drinkstone, passing the Bear Inn on your left. After some 450 yards, turn right along a waymarked path, following it into an open field, with a hedgerow on the left. Soon the path crosses into the field on the left: continue straight ahead, but now with the hedgerow on your right. At the end of the field the path passes to the right of a house with wicker fencing and continues into the churchyard. Turn left and pass behind **All Saints' Church** and go out through the front gate.

      Continue along the track opposite the front gate, passing Beyton Garage on your left. The track becomes a path and then narrows as it passes between hedgerows. Continue along it as it opens out on the right, following it to reach a metalled lane (Quaker Lane). Cross the lane and follow the path opposite, with Quaker's Farm on your left. After a few yards you will reach a metal gate: go through and bear slightly right, heading between two trees in the corner of a small field. Go into the adjacent field and cross to the far side to reach the edge of Chevin's Woods. Turn left and follow the edge of the woods, with an open field on your left. At the end of the field, go into the field with woodland still on your right. Just after the end of the woods, walk on to the end of the field and then turn right to go along a wider track, with a hedgerow on your left. Follow the track to a metalled lane. Turn right along the lane, passing High House on your left.

After following the lane for some 350 yards, take a waymarked path on the right. Go over a sleeper bridge and follow the path as it bears slightly left towards the corner of the woods in the distance. Bear left and continue around the edge of the field to reach a metalled lane (Quaker's Lane again). Turn right and follow the lane for about 250 yards, then turn left along a track into an arable field. Walk along the right-hand edge of the field, then turn left, and then right, to reach a metalled road (Bury Road). Turn right and follow the road back to Beyton and the White Horse.

POINTS OF INTEREST:

All Saints' Church, Beyton – This part-Norman church is noted for having one of only four round buttressed towers in West Suffolk. Unfortunately the church is kept locked, but access can be obtained from one of the keyholders listed in the church porch.

REFRESHMENTS:
The White Horse, Beyton.
The Bear Inn, Beyton.

Walk 8 THORNHAM PARVA 3¹/₂m (5¹/₂km)

Maps: OS Sheets Landranger 156; Pathfinder 964.

A walk to a 14th-century thatched church.

Start: At 108715, the Field Studies Centre car park, Thornham Magna.

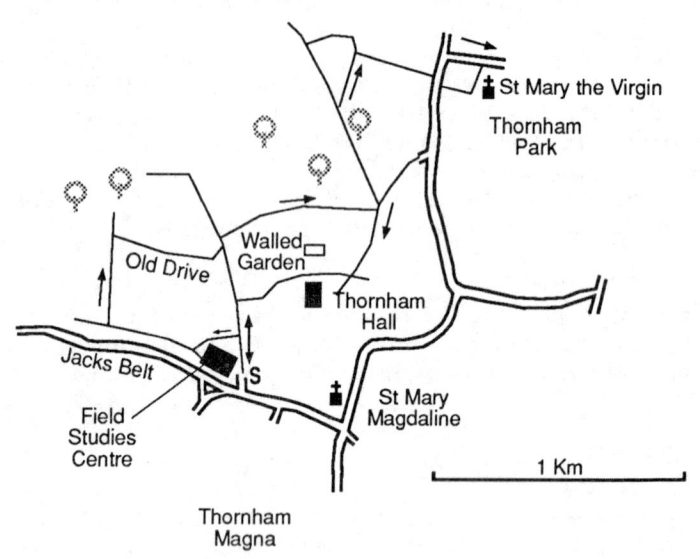

From the **Thornham Estate** Field Studies Centre car park, follow the path past the gift shop and, ignoring the track off to the left (to the Visitor's Centre), carry straight on to reach a stile on the left. Cross into the horse's field (Hobby Close) and head towards the hedge on the left-hand side of the field. Follow the hedge to the corner of the field and cross a stile into Queen Elizabeth Copse, planted in 1982 to commemorate the 80th birthday of Queen Elizabeth the Queen Mother.

Follow the path through the plantation, turning right at the end to follow a track into an open field. Now follow the left-hand edge of the field, with a small plantation (Jack's Belt) on your left. At the end of the field, turn right along a track, following it up to the woodland at the top of the hill. Once in the wood, take the track on your right (Old Drive), following it through the wood to reach a junction of tracks. Turn left and, after a few yards, before an open field, turn right along a track. Continue along the track, with a poplar plantation on your left, passing a track on the right, to reach a T-junction of tracks, with an open field in front of you. Turn left and, after some 400 yards, turn right along a path, with a ditch on your right. At the end of the woodland, turn right into an open field, and then go left to follow the edge of the field to another wood. Continue along the path to reach a metalled lane opposite the thatched **Thornham Parva Church.**

Turn left, and then after a few yards, turn right to follow the lane past the old vicarage, on your left. Take the next right to reach the church. From the back of the church, take the path on the right, going through a gate to rejoin the metalled lane used earlier. Turn left, and then, soon, right to go along the driveway to Thornham Hall. Just as the driveway bears to the left, take the track that goes straight on and then turn left to go down to the 'Walks Car Park'. Turn left in front of the wall and follow the path, going right at the end of the wall. Keep straight on along the path, glimpsing Thornham Hall through the trees on the left. Now follow the gravelled path back to the Field Studies Centre car park.

POINTS OF INTEREST:

Thornham Estate – The estate has been owned by the Henniker family since 1756. The present Lord and Lady Henniker opened up the estate for educational and recreational purposes and to provide local employment. The estate now combines a working farm, with forestry, shooting and workshops. There are also several circular walks and a Field Studies Centre.

St Mary's Church, Thornham Parva – This is an entirely thatched church which contains a rare 14th-century retable depicting the Crucifixion. The retable was discovered by Lord Henniker in 1927 in his stables and is known to have been purchased by one of his ancestors in 1778 from Rookery Farm, Stradbroke.

REFRESHMENTS:

There is a tea room beside the car park at the start/finish of the walk.

Walk 9   **EYE** $3^{1}/_{2}$m ($5^{1}/_{2}$km)

Maps: OS Sheets Landranger 156; Pathfinder 964.

A walk around a delightful Suffolk rural town.

Start: At 143736, the Community Centre car park, Eye.

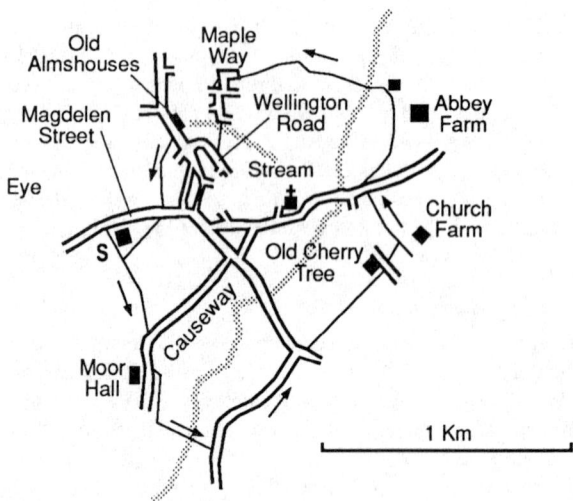

From the car park, cross the entrance driveway, go over a wooden bridge and enter Town Moors. Take a few minutes to roam around the area with its interesting sculptors and memorials to the great storm.

    To continue the walk, turn left and follow the path on the left-hand edge of Town Moors, following it over a sleeper bridge and then along a line of the electricity poles. Go over a second sleeper bridge and past a pond on the right. Soon you join a path, on the right, that takes you out of Town Moors, over a concrete bridge and into an arable field with a ditch on your left. After a few yards you will reach a track (Moorhall Causeway): turn right and follow the track round to the front of Moor Hall. Cross a stile on the left and follow the right-hand side of the field beyond, in front of the Hall, to reach the field corner. Now bear right to head for a stile and bridge over a ditch at

22

the bottom of the field. Cross the stile and ditch and continue in roughly the same direction, going over two further stiles to reach a metal gate. Go through the gate and turn left to go down a green lane (Park Lane).

Follow this raised lane past meadows, on your left, to reach to a metalled road. Cross the road and follow the track opposite to reach a stile into a paddock. Cross the stile and follow the right-hand edge of the paddock to reach another stile. Cross and follow the path beyond, going between houses to reach a road (Ludgate Causeway).

Turn left and, just before the Old Cherry Tree public house (now closed), turn right along a footpath towards Church Farm. When you reach the concrete driveway to the farm, turn left and follow the drive to the Hoxne Road. Cross the road and go up the driveway opposite to Abbey Farm. Pass **Abbey Farmhouse**, on the right, and then go through the farmyard. Soon you bear left, past a new cottage, on your right, to continue along a track. Go over a stile and then a bridge over the River Dove and maintain direction, going up the left-hand side of a large field. At the top of the hill, cross the stile on the left and continue along the right-hand side of the field beyond, heading towards a housing estate.

Follow the path into a parking area and bear right to return to **Eye**, going down Maple Way. Where Maple Way turns to the left, keep roughly straight on, going along a path that soon brings you out to a T-junction. Continue straight down the turning opposite and go over a bridge into Wellington Road. Turn right and, at the junction with Lambseth Street, turn right again. Now, within a few yards, turn left down a trackway in front of the old Almshouses. Keep straight on into a wood and, where the path divides, bear left to go uphill. Follow the path to reach Magdalen Street. Cross the road and take the path opposite, going down to the side of the Community Centre and so back to the car park.

POINTS OF INTEREST:
Abbey Farmhouse – The house is part of an 11th-century priory and still contains parts of the original structure.
Eye – There are many fine buildings in Eye, of special interest being the Guildhall, Church and Castle Mound. To get the best out of a visit to the town, buy a copy of the booklet on the town history.

REFRESHMENTS:
There are several possibilities in Eye.

Walk 10   **WORTHAM COMMON** $3\frac{1}{2}$m ($5\frac{1}{2}$km)

Maps: OS Sheets Landranger 144; Pathfinder 964.

A walk across Suffolk heath land.

Start: At 098793, the car park on Wortham Common.

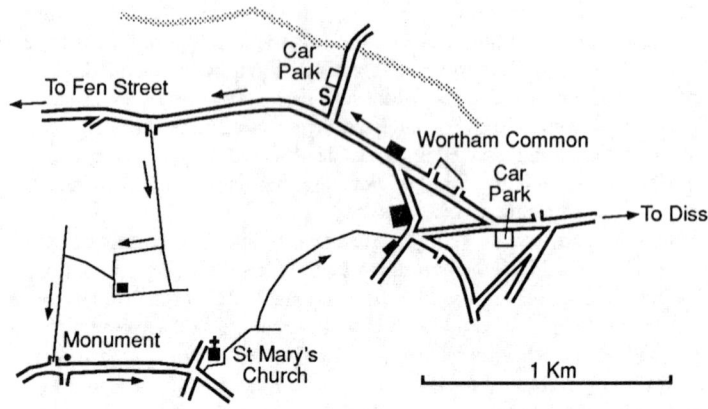

There are several car parks on Wortham Common and any one can be used on this walk. The common has many ill-defined paths and it is suggested that you use the indicated map to find your way to where the walk leaves the Common.

Leave the common and join the road to Fen Street. After leaving the common, and just opposite the first cottage on the right, take a track on the left, following it up a slight hill between hedgerows. At the top of the hill, continue along the track until you come to the end of the field on your right. Now turn right into the field and walk along its left-hand edge, with a hedgerow on your left. (This path may not be very distinct).

The path soon leads into a large open field: turn left and, after some 100 yards, turn right along a track. Follow the track to its junction with a further track. There, turn left and follow a line of electricity poles down to a metalled road. On the corner here there is a plaque commemorating one of the many incidences that took place in the **'tithe war'**.

Turn left along the metalled road, following it to **St Mary's Church.** From the back, right-hand side of the church, follow a path through a kissing gate and bear right across a small pasture to reach a stile. Cross the stile and walk to the corner of the field beyond. Cross two further stiles to reach a plantation. Bear left, keeping the hedgerow on your left and the plantation on your right. Follow the hedgerow to the end of the plantation, and then go down the left-hand edge of another field. Turn left in the corner of this field to go along an overgrown path. Follow the path between houses to reach a metalled road. You are now back on Wortham Common: follow your map to return to the starting car park.

POINTS OF INTEREST:

Tithe Wars – During the 1920s and 1930s many farmers were still expected to pay tithes to the church, although very few of them were members of their local congregation. The tithes were based on pre-war corn values and with depressed prices in the 1920s many farmers refused to pay. As a result the 'Commissioners of Queen Ann's Bounty' seized livestock to auction them in order to redeem the tithe money. Civil unrest followed, this only being curtailed by the start of the World War II.

St Mary's Church – The church is noted for having the largest Norman round tower in England (29 foot in diameter). The top of the tower unfortunately collapsed in 1780 and is still in a state of disrepair.

REFRESHMENTS:

There are no refreshments at Wortham Common or en route. The nearest are to be found in Diss, a short distance north-eastwards.

Walk 11   EASTON PARK $3^{1}/_{2}$m ($5^{1}/_{2}$km)

Maps: OS Sheets Landranger 156; Pathfinder 1008.

A walk around Easton Park and the Crinkle-Crankle wall.

Start: At 283586, the car park opposite the White Horse, Easton.

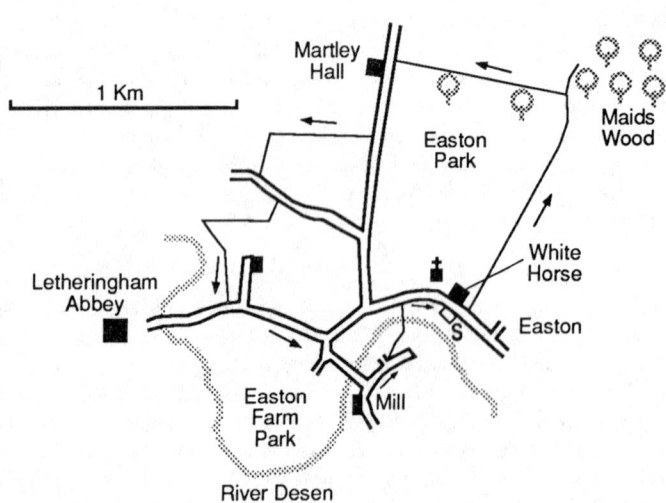

From the car park in **Easton**, turn right and walk along the road for about 70 yards and then turn left up a small waymarked track. The track soon leads up to the cricket ground: cross by keeping to the left-hand edge, ignoring the 'Private' signs. At the end of the cricket field, keep straight on, with an arable field to your right and woods to your left, following the path to its end at Maids Wood. Turn left and follow a path along the left-hand side of another arable field to reach the field corner. Now keep straight on, going over a small ditch and sleeper bridge and along the side of another field to reach a metalled road.

Turn left along the road, passing Martley Hall. About 300 yards further on, take the waymarked path on the right, going down the right-hand side of an arable field. Go through a gap in the hedge and continue to the next field corner. Go through another hedge and turn left along a waymarked path down the left-hand side of a field to reach a road. In the distance to the right on this section of the walk, you can see the buildings of Letheringham Abbey.

Turn left along the road and, after some 100 yards, turn right into a field. Follow the path (not waymarked), keeping the hedge to your right, to reach a drainage ditch flowing into the River Deben. Now keep to the edge of the field to reach a stile. Cross the stile and turn right along the edge of a pasture to reach another stile. Cross to reach a road. Turn left along the road, with Easton Farm Park clearly visible on your right. Walk along the road for some 500 yards to reach a road junction. Bear right past the entrance to **Easton Farm Park**. Continue along the road, going over the River Deben. After a further 100 yards, turn left along a gravel lane. Carry straight on here if you wish to visit **Letheringham Mill**.

Just before the driveway to a private house, turn left, go over a stile and follow a pleasant, tree-lined path over the River Deben, passing the Easton Harriers Kennels on your right. Continue to reach a road. Turn right, passing All Saints' Church and the White Horse, on your left. Continue along the road to return to the car park.

POINTS OF INTEREST:

Easton – The village of Easton was the seat of the Duke of Hamilton, but is now renown for the Crinkle-Crankle wall around Easton Park. The wall is constructed in an undulating fashion to provide the required strength with fewer bricks. Sadly, with the wall in partial decay, it has not been strong enough.

Easton Farm Park – This is a popular place for families to spend the day. The farm's attractions include prize-winning Suffolk Punch horses and a Pet's Paddock where visitors can feed the animals.

Letheringham Mill – This 18th-century watermill has been fully restored and is open to the public on Sundays and Bank Holiday Mondays during the summer. Tel: 01728 746349 for exact times. Refreshments are also available.

REFRESHMENTS:

The White Horse, Easton.

Refreshments are also available to visitors to Easton Farm Park and Letheringham Mill.

Walk 12   **KNETTISHALL HEATH**   3¹/₂m (5¹/₂km)

Maps: OS Sheets Landranger 144; Pathfinder 943.

A walk around the Country Park.

Start: At 955807, the main car park on Knettishall Heath.

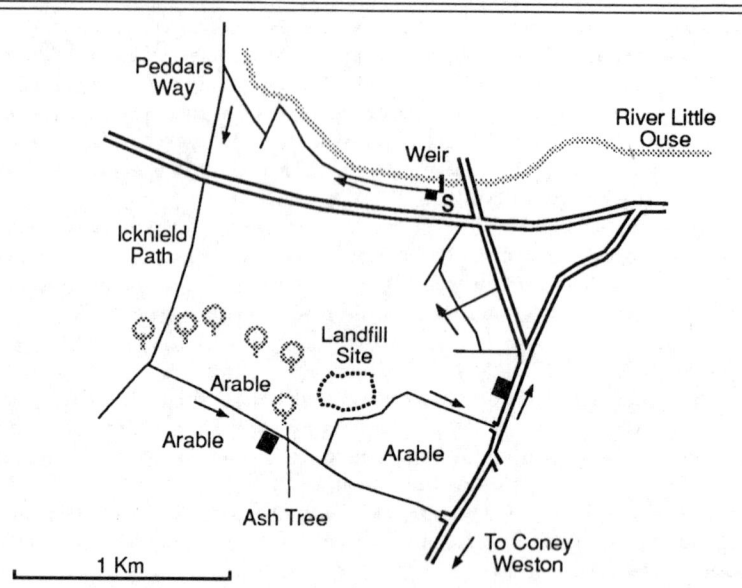

From the Country Park's car park, go to the right-hand side of the toilet block and continue down to the edge of the River Little Ouse, reaching it next to the weir. Turn left and follow the river bank down to the end of the field. Follow the path as it turns left and heads for a wooden bridge over a ditch. On the far side, turn right and follow the path through woodland to reach a main track opposite an old birch tree. You are now on **Peddar's Way**, part of an old trackway leading to the Norfolk coast.

Turn left and follow the track to a metalled lane. Cross the lane and walk through a car park. Now go along another track, part of the **Icknield Way** long distance path which follows an ancient trackway all the way to Dorset. Continue along the track, soon leaving the Country Park. Soon, you will reach an arable field on the left. Turn left at a waymarker and follow a cross-field track, heading for an ash tree and cottage in the distance.

28

Just beyond the cottage, turn left along a track, soon bearing right next to a landfill site. Walk down to an open field and turn left there to follow a track along its left-hand edge. Soon, the track turns right: follow it to reach a metalled lane. Turn left along the lane, passing a cottage on the left and continuing to reach a road junction. There, leave the road, turning left along a track into the woods. Follow the track to reach its junction with a path to the right. Turn right and follow the path, initially through birch trees. Continue along the path, soon crossing two other paths. When the path meets a major track coming in from the left, bear right and follow the track, soon bearing left to reach a metalled lane. Cross the lane to reach the starting car park on Knettishall Heath.

POINTS OF INTEREST:

Peddar's Way – The combination of Peddar's Way and the Norfolk Coast Path is one of Britain's official National Trails. Peddar's Way follows a Romanised section of the ancient Icknield Way, meeting the coast at Holme-next-the-Sea. The Norfolk Coast Path starts at Hunstanton, soon joining Peddar's Way and continuing to Cromer.

Icknield Way – This 103 mile route links Knettishall Heath to Ivinghoe Beacon in Buckinghamshire following the line of the prehistoric route. At Ivinghoe Beacon it links with the Ridgeway Path National Trail which ends near Avebury. From there, the Wessex Path continues to Swanage in Dorset.

Knettishall Heath – The heath has been designated a Site of Special Scientific Interest (SSSI) by English Nature. It consists of 375 acres of heathland, a remnant of that which was once found all over Breckland. The area's woodland is typical of scrub and tree encroachment that occurs if heathland is left unmanaged. The heath is the terminus for three long distance walks, the two mentioned above and Angles Way, a 78 mile route along the River Waveney to Great Yarmouth.

REFRESHMENTS:

There are no refreshments at Knettishall Heath. The nearest inn is the Swan at Coney Weston about 2 miles to the south.

Walk 13   **FARNHAM**   3$\frac{1}{2}$m (5$\frac{1}{2}$km)

Maps: OS Sheets Landranger 156; Pathfinder 1008.

A pleasant walk past woods and heath.

Start: At 363599, St Mary's Church, Farnham.

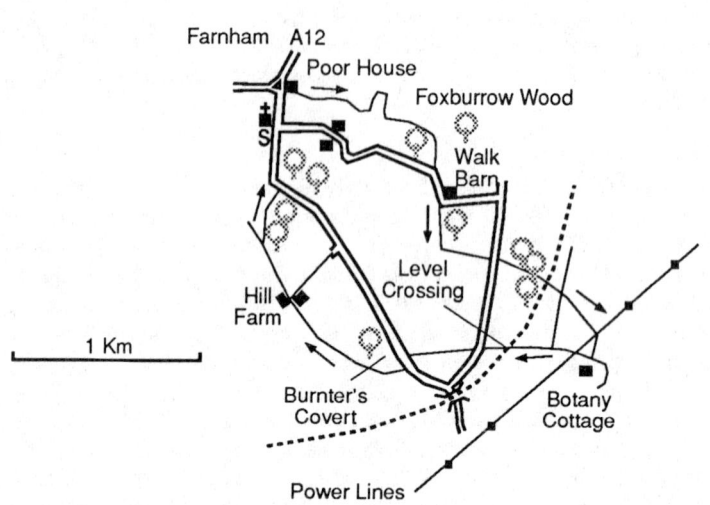

From the church, walk back towards the main road (the A12) and, at the bottom of the hill, turn right in front of the Old Poor House to follow a path which goes up into a pasture. Continue to the corner of the field and go through a small wood. Go along the right-hand edge of the next field to reach a stile on the right. Cross the stile and the small pasture beyond to reach another stile. Turn left and go around the edge of the next arable field to reach the edge of Foxburrow Wood.

Turn left and follow the edge of the wood to reach a metalled lane. Bear left and follow the lane down to Walk Barn. Now, where the lane turns left, go straight on, walking along the edge of a narrow plantation. At the end of the plantation, go over a stile and turn left to follow a path out to a metalled lane. Cross the lane and keep straight on through woodland to reach a level crossing. Cross the tracks, with care, and continue along the path on the other side. When the path reaches a sandy track, keep straight on along the edge of a field and then turn right to head towards a barn underneath the power lines. Just beyond the barn, turn right and go along a track in front of Botany Cottage.

Follow the track back to the railway and another level crossing. Cross the railway tracks, again with care, and follow the path beyond to a road. Cross and go straight on, following a path to reach another road. Turn left, and follow the road for about 200 yards to reach a left-hand bend. There, turn right and go along a track. Follow the track, with Burnter's Covert on your right, to reach Hill Farm. Go through the farm, with the farmhouse on your right, continuing along the track. Now, where the track bears left, bear right along an indistinct path to the left-hand side of a small wood. Follow this path to some steps leading down to a metalled lane. Turn left to follow the lane back to **St Mary's Church, Farnham**.

POINTS OF INTEREST:
St Mary's Church, Farnham – The church was built on the site of a Roman encampment. The chancel is of Norman origin, but the tower and roof are Tudor.

REFRESHMENTS:
The George and Dragon, Farnham.

Maps: OS Sheets Landranger 143 and 154; Pathfinder 962.
A walk from Mildenhall along the River Lark.
Start: At 713746, the main car park in Mildenhall.

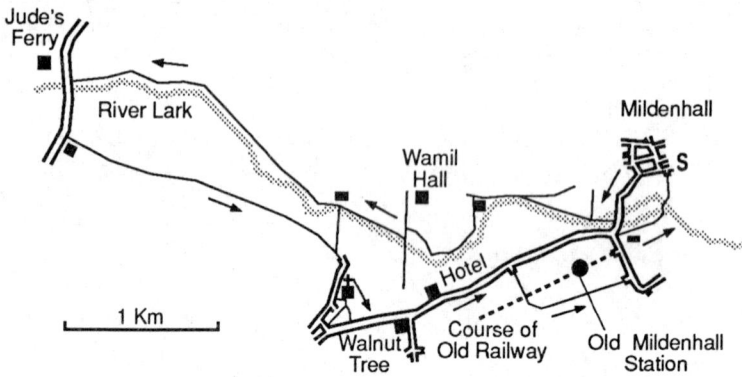

From the car park go down St Andrew's Street and turn left into Mill Street. Go down
Mill Street, passing the Riverside Hotel on the left, to reach the bridge over the River
Lark. Turn right and follow the river, with it on your left hand, soon crossing a bridge
over a mill stream. Continue beside the river until, after some 800 yards, you reach a
small cottage on the left. Immediately beyond the cottage, turn left down the left-
hand side of an arable field to return to the river. Now resume walking beside the
river, still with it on your left hand, to reach a driveway leading to Wamil Hall. Cross
the driveway and continue beside the river. Soon you will reach a stile. Cross this stile
into an adjacent arable field and follow its left-hand edge, with the river still on your
left, to reach an isolated house. Go through a kissing gate and follow the river's edge,
with the house on your right.

The shorter walk crosses the bridge on the left and follows the path beyond to reach a gap in the scrub. Go through the scrub and then turn left to rejoin the longer route.

The longer walk crosses rougher terrain: go through a second kissing gate and follow the riverbank to reach the bridge at West Row. The Jude's Ferry is to the right. Turn left over the bridge, and follow the road. Now, after some 200 yards, bear left to follow a bridleway in front of a farm building. Continue along the bridleway for just over a mile to rejoin the shorter route coming in from the left.

The route now maintains the direction of the longer walk to reach a barn on the right. Turn right here and follow the lane to All Saint's Church, Worlington. Turn left into the churchyard, pass to the right of the church and then turn right behind Church Cottage. Now turn left into the cemetery and go along its right-hand edge to reach a wooden bridge. Go over the bridge and follow the path beyond, then turn left into the High Street. Go along the High Street, passing the Walnut Tree on your right. Continue along the Worlington Road towards Mildenhall and then, after some 800 yards, turn right over a stile and follow the cross-field track beyond. The track soon crosses the route of the old Cambridge to Mildenhall branch of the Great Eastern Railway: continue along the track, but soon turn left along a waymarked path. On the left you now have a fine view of the old **Mildenhall Station** and platform. Continue along the path to reach Station Road. Turn left and follow the road to a junction. Here, turn sharp right to go along a driveway, with the river and a weir on your left. Soon you will reach a wooden bridge on your left: cross and continue to cross a second bridge. The path beyond bears left and returns to the car park and the start of the walk.

POINTS OF INTEREST:

Mildenhall Station – The station was the terminus of the Cambridge to Mildenhall branch of the Great Eastern Railway. Built in 1884, the line was closed to passenger traffic in 1962 and to freight traffic in 1965. The station is now a private residence.

REFRESHMENTS:

The Jude's Ferry, West Row.
The Walnut Tree, Worlington.
The Worlington Hall Country House Hotel, Worlington.
There are also numerous possibilities in Mildenhall.

Maps: OS Sheets Landranger 169; Pathfinder 1031,
A walk across heathland and past the Sutton Hoo burial ground.
Start: At 298491, the car park next to the road junction of the
Orford and Bawdsey roads.

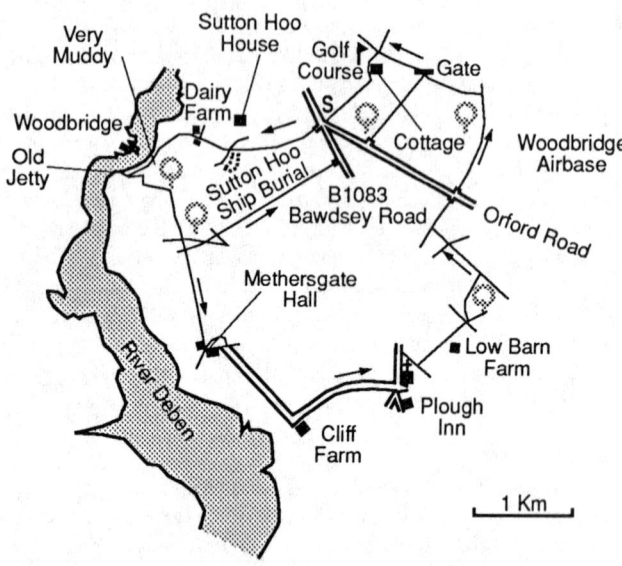

Leave the car park, cross the Bawdsey road (the B1083), with care, and follow the
sandy track opposite the road junction. Follow the track, with trees on the right and
grass on the left, to reach a junction of tracks. Go straight on, now with Sutton Hoo
House on the right and the **Anglo-Saxon burial ground** on the left. At the next junction
of tracks, bear right, downhill, and then bear right again, passing Little Sutton Hoo on
the left. Just beyond a bend in the track, turn left into Dairy Farm. Go to the left of a
bungalow and continue along the path past a new pump house, on the left, to reach the
bank of the River Deben. Turn left and follow the river bank to the old ferry jetty.
There, turn left and follow the left-hand edge of a field to reach woodland at the top of

34

the hill. Continue around the field edge, with the woods on your left, until you reach a cross-field path leading away from the corner of the wood. Follow this path across the field to reach the track opposite.

The shorter walk turns left here, following the track to the main road (the B1083). Turn left along the road, with care, for some 400 yards to return to the start.

The longer walk crosses the track and follows the track opposite to Methersgate Hall. Turn right, and then left to follow the track to the side of the Hall. Turn left through a white gate in the fence and walk in front of the Hall, continuing along a driveway. At a junction, turn right to go along a now-metalled driveway, passing Cliff Farm, on the right, and continuing to reach the main road (the B1083). The Plough is to the right here. Turn left and follow the road, with care, for some 200 yards, passing Church Farm on the right. Turn right down a byway and, after 200 yards, turn left to go along a concrete driveway, passing Low Barn Farm on your right, and continuing to reach a junction of tracks. Bear left to follow a waymarked path towards a pine plantation. Bear left to follow the edge of the plantation and, at the corner of the plantation, turn right to continue along the edge. Soon you will reach a trackway: turn left and follow this track, through birch/pine woodland, until you come out to heathland again at a wooden gate. Turn right along a track to reach a main road (the Orford road) opposite Woodbridge Airfield. Cross and follow the track opposite for about 1,000 yards, passing the end of the runway on your right and continuing to the end of the plantation on your left. Now turn left and continue along a track for another 1,000 yards to where it bends to the left. There, continue straight on along a waymarked path. After a few yards, go through a gate on the left on to Woodbridge Golf Course and continue along the bridleway, soon passing the 7th tee. At the end of the fairway on your left, turn left to pass to the right-hand side of a cottage. Now bear left to reach the left-hand side of the golf course and then follow the line of a fence down to a gate. Go through the gate and follow the track beyond back to the car park and the start of the walk.

POINTS OF INTEREST:
Sutton Hoo Anglo-Saxon Burial Ground – This is one of the most famous archaeological sites in the country. Excavations in 1939 revealed the richest burial in Britain – an Anglo-Saxon burial ship with all its treasure. The burial is believed to be that of King Raedwald who ruled East Anglia from 599 to 624/5 AD. The site is open to the public on weekend afternoons from April to September.

REFRESHMENTS:
The Plough, Sutton.

Walk 18　　　　　　　**SOUTHWOLD**　　　　　4m (6$\frac{1}{2}$km)

Maps: OS Sheets Landranger 156; Pathfinder 966.

An easy short walk around the outskirts of Southwold.

Start: At 512770, the sea front car park, Southwold.

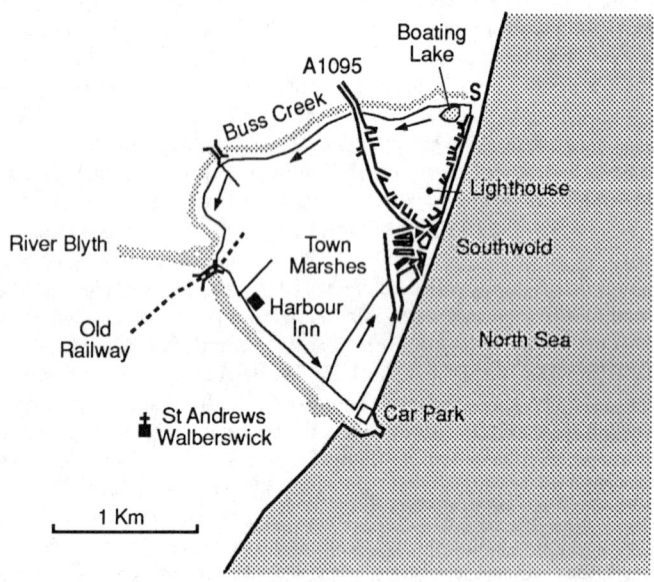

From the car park, head inland, passing to the right of a boating lake as you follow a very clear path on top of an embankment. The path soon follows the left-hand side of Buss Creek: continue along it to reach the main road (the A1092) by a road bridge. Cross the road, with care, and continue along the left-hand side of the creek, passing two small bridges on the right and an embankment on the left. Soon you will reach a stile with a path going both to the left and the right. Cross the stile, and then a second stile, and continue straight on, following the side of the creek as it bears left. In the distance you can now see St Andrew's Church, Walberswick and, on the horizon to the right, Blythburgh Church.

The path passes beside Buss Creek grazing marsh, then soon passes a disused wind pump, on your right, and a sluice gate. Continue along it to reach an iron bridge, on your right, crossing the River Blyth. This bridge replaced the original swing bridge that carried the Southwold Light Railway over the river. This narrow gauge railway was opened in 1879 and carried mainly fish, coal, grain and milk as well as passengers from Southwold to the main line at Halesworth. The line was eventually closed in 1929.

Continue along the riverside, going past a group of houses, the Harbour Inn and various small huts. After 700 yards, take a waymarked path on the left, following it down the edge of Town Marsh. Continue along the path to return to **Southwold**. Once you are back in the town, go up Constitution Hill to reach South Green. Now either wander through the town or follow the cliff top path back to the car park.

POINTS OF INTEREST:

Southwold – This quiet seaside town has many fine buildings from the Georgian and Victorian eras. In order to do justice to these buildings it is recommend that the walker buy a copy of *Discovering Southwold* published jointly by the Southwold and Reydon Society and the Suffolk Preservation Society. It is very reasonably priced and obtainable from bookshops in the town. Further information can be obtained from the Town Hall, next to the Swan Hotel. Two buildings in Southwold pre-date the disastrous fire of 1659 that destroyed most of the town and are especially worth visiting. Sutherland House was the headquarters of the Duke of York at the time of the Battle of Sole Bay in 1672 and still has an original 16th-century plaster ceiling. It is now a restaurant. St Edmund's Church was built in the 15th century to replace the original church built in 1202 and subsequently destroyed by fire in the reign of Henry IV.

REFRESHMENTS:

There are numerous possibilities in Southwold. The Harbour Inn, which is about halfway around the walk, is particularly worth considering.

Walk 19 CLARE AND THE STOUR VALLEY RAILWAY 4m (6½km)
Maps: OS Sheets Landranger 155; Pathfinder 1028.
A gentle walk past Clare Castle and along part of the old railway.
Start: At 771452, the car park in Clare Country Park.

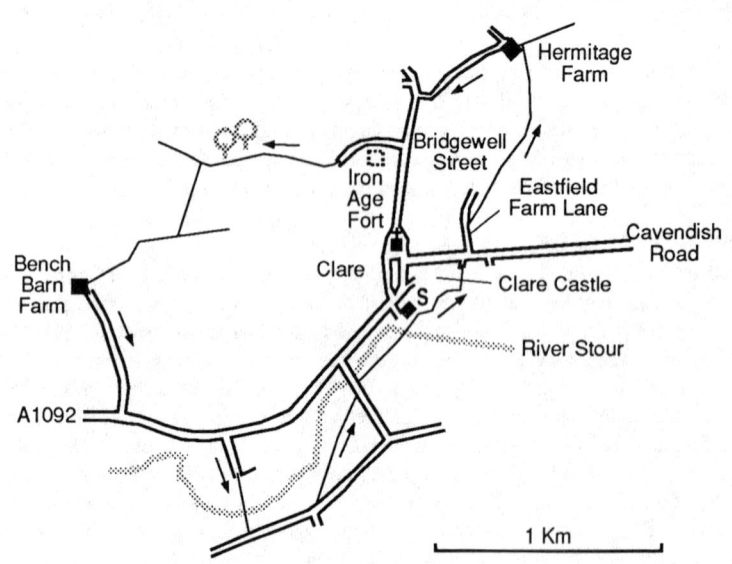

From the car park head to the left of the **old station** goods shed and bear left towards the **Castle**. Here you can take a diversion to see the Norman keep. To continue, take the path signposted Lady's Walk, go up some steps and then down to the far side of the castle. Turn left over a ditch and then bear right towards the children's play area. Now follow the path out to Cavendish Road. Turn right and, soon, left along Eastfield Farm Lane. Go to the right of a poultry house and out to arable fields, following the path until it divides by an electricity pole. Bear left and follow a path towards Hermitage Farm. At the farm turn left and follow the lane down to the main road (Bridgewell Street).

Turn left along the road, but, after some 250 yards, turn right to go up an old track (Sheepgate Lane), passing Clare Camp (an Iron Age fort) on your left. At the top of the hill, keep straight on past outbuildings, on your left, and then a copse, on your right. At the next hill top, turn left and then, after 400 yards, go right, heading down towards Bench Barn Farm. Follow the lane from the farm to the main road (the A1092).

Turn left and, after 500 yards, turn right – crossing the road with care – to follow a track to the golf course. At the end of the track, cross the footbridge over the River Stour and then turn left at a junction with a metalled lane. Just past the next road junction on the right, turn left along a waymarked path, going through gates and down the side of a garden. At the bottom of the garden, turn right through a gate and follow a ditch. Continue along the backs of gardens and then the edge of a field to reach a main road. Turn left towards the centre of **Clare**, and then right, just before a bridge, to follow the old railway track back to the car park.

POINTS OF INTEREST:

Clare Station – The Stour Valley Railway was built by the Great Eastern Railway Company and opened in 1865. It saw its best days before World War I. During the 1920s traffic remained high, but during World War II the line was mainly used for freight purposes. After the war the line was never economic and it finally closed in 1967.

Clare Castle – The manor of Clare was given to Richard Fitzgilbert by William the Conqueror for services at the Battle of Hastings. Fitzgilbert became the first Lord of Clare and began building the castle at the end of the 11th century. In 1314 the last of the de Clare family was killed at the Battle of Bannockburn and three generations later the castle fell into disrepair. Little of the castle remains today save for the Norman keep which can be viewed.

Clare – There are many fine buildings in the village, some dating from the 14th century. Some of the finest are the Ancient House, The Grove, Chapel Cottage, Nethergate Hotel and Stour House. The Church of St Peter and St Paul is of unknown origin, but has many fine features, particularly the 13th- and 14th-century tower with its peal of eight bells (the oldest dating from 1400).

REFRESHMENTS:

There are plenty of opportunities in Clare.

Walk 20   **NAYLAND**   4m (6$\frac{1}{2}$km)

Maps: OS Sheets Landranger 155; Pathfinder 1052.

A walk through the town and along the River Stour.

Start: At 973340, the lay-by by the bridge next to the Anchor Inn.

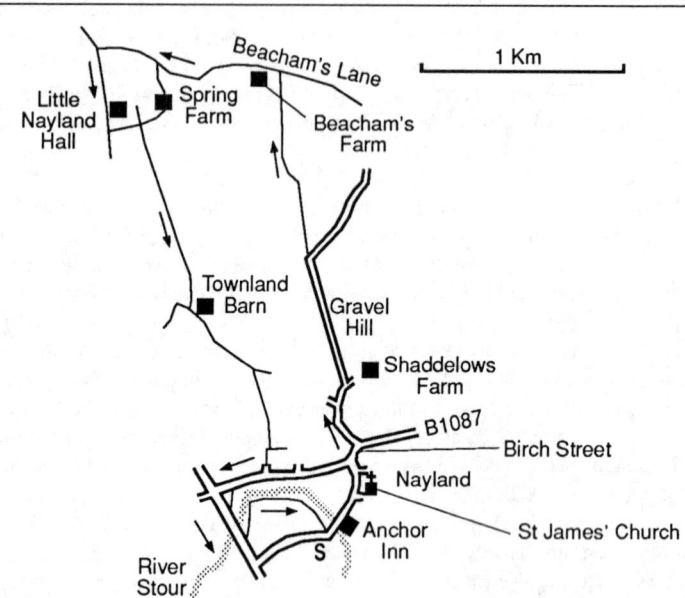

From the lay-by go over the bridge, passing the Anchor Inn on your left, and along the High Street. At the junction with Birch Street, turn right and then left into Gravel Hill. Walk up Gravel Hill, past Shaddelows Farm on your right, and, after about 900 yards, where the road bends sharp right, keep straight on along a very pleasant old track (Farthings Lane), passing old hawthorn and holly hedgerows. Where the track opens out into a field, bear left and follow the edge of the field, eventually going down steps to reach Beachams Lane. Turn left and follow the lane past Beachams Farm and up a slope to reach a road junction (Spring Farm is on your left).

Bear right and follow the lane to the next junction. Turn left and follow a track, passing Little Nayland Hall on your left. Just past the Hall, at the bottom of a small hill, take the footpath on the left, going over a stile and along the right-hand side of two fields to reach another stile. Go over this stile and turn right to follow the right-hand side of the field. Now go down a slope to reach a stile and cross it into a small wood. Go through the wood and then keep straight on to reach Townland Barn.

Walk in front of the 'Barn', go through a copse and then down a hill. Go through a gap in the hedge and cross to a paddock. Go through the paddock, heading towards a stile just past a farm gate on the left-hand side. Follow the path beyond past a cemetery to reach a metalled lane. Bear right along this lane, heading down into **Nayland**. Turn right along Bear Street to reach an open green and the River Stour. Now take a path along the riverside to reach a bridge. Cross and turn immediately left to follow the riverside past a weir and back to the lay-by and the **Anchor Inn,** by the next bridge.

POINTS OF INTEREST:

Nayland – This attractive village was once the 45th largest town in England. It thrived on the wool trade and many signs of its glorious past can still be seen to day. The village church, dedicated to St James, is best known for its altar piece – 'Christ blessing the wine at the Last Supper' – which was painted by John Constable. This is one of only two sacred paintings painted by Constable.

Anchor Inn – Just behind the inn is Court Knoll, an ancient settlement site where the original Manor stood. The moated field can still be seen.

REFRESHMENTS:

The Anchor Inn, Nayland.

There are also other opportunities in the village.

Walk 21   THE WALDINGFIELDS   4m (6½km)

Maps: OS Sheets Landranger 155; Pathfinder 1029.
A circular walk along well-defined paths.
Start: At 924451, St Lawrence's Church, Little Waldingfield.

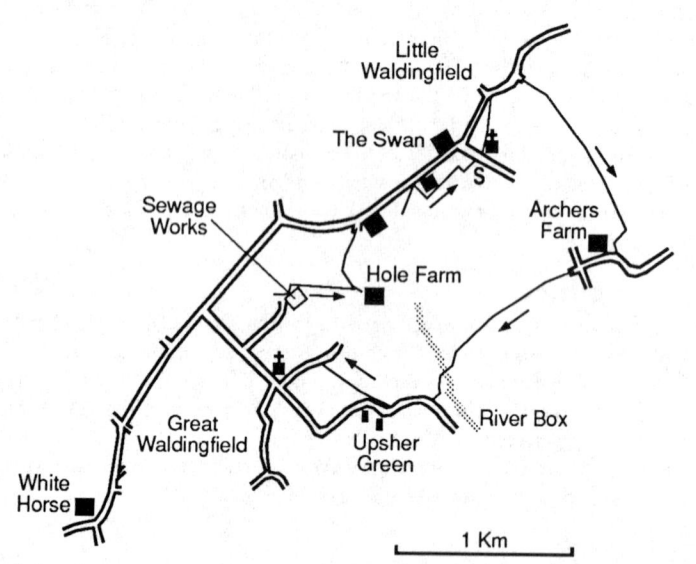

Parking is possible in the street close to the church, but please park thoughtfully.

    Take the path to the left of the church, going around to the back and following the path past the new cemetery. The path continues across an open field to reach the Monks Eleigh to Little Waldingfield Road. Turn right along the road, but after 200 yards turn right again, just past a house, on to a track. Follow a track until it peters out and becomes a path continuing in the same direction. At the top of a slope the path joins the corner of a hedge: go through the hedge, over a small bridge and turn right to continue to a T-junction beside Archers Farm.

    Turn right, passing the farm and continuing to a T-junction. Cross the road and continue along the track opposite, with Great Waldingfield Church straight ahead and Little Waldingfield Church to the right. The track soon becomes a path leading down the left-hand side of a field to reach a small bridge. Cross the bridge and then cross another bridge over the River Box. Turn left and follow the edge of a field to reach a road. Turn right along the road passing through the hamlet of Upsher Green.

Just past the last house on the right, take a path, also on the right, following it to a metalled lane. Turn left and follow the lane up to a T-junction. Turn right to reach Great Waldingfield Church. The road almost opposite the church will take you down to Great Waldingfield for a visit to the White Horse if lunch or drinks are required.

The walk continues past the church. Take a metalled track on your right, following it past the sewage treatment works. The track then becomes a path: follow it around a pasture to reach a driveway. Turn left and follow the driveway to a road. Turn right and either follow the road into Little Waldingfield for refreshments at the Swan Inn, or take a path, on the right just before the village sign, and follow it past the allotments to return to **Little Waldingfield Church**.

POINTS OF INTEREST:
Little Waldingfield Church – St Lawrence's Church, built in the 15th century, has fine brasses dating from 1506, a Jacobean pulpit and 15th-century font.

REFRESHMENTS:
The Swan, Little Waldingfield.
The White Horse, Great Waldingfield.
Supplies can also be bought at the Post Office in Great Waldingfield.

Maps: OS Sheets Landranger 155; Pathfinder 1029.
A walk by Nedging Mill and the River Brett.
Start: At 992494, the car park in Market Square, Bildeston.

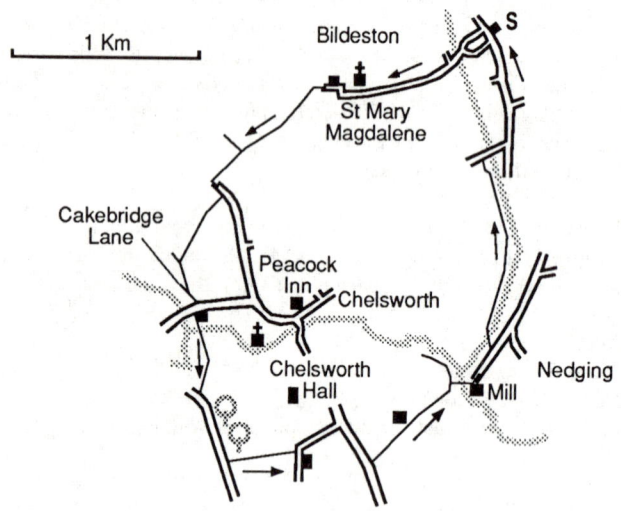

From the car park, go down Chapel Street and turn left into Church Road. Follow the lane, past the **Church of St Mary Magdalene** on the right and then past a house and pond on the left. At end of the track turn left to go along the left-hand side of a field, with a hedge on your left. At the end of the field, go over a small bridge and maintain direction along the left-hand edge of the next field to reach the end of a track. Turn left, then, after a few yards, turn right to go across an open field towards a gap in the distant woods. Go through the gap and head down to another track.

Turn right, and then left to cross a ditch. Now head for the left-hand side of a thatched cottage, keeping a hedge on your right. At the cottage, drop down on to a green lane (Cakebridge Lane) and follow this, somewhat wet, lane to a road. Turn right along the road, and then left just before a bridge to walk with a stream on your right and a house on your left. At the back of the house, cross a bridge and a stile, and then maintain direction to reach a metalled road. Turn left, up the road, and then left again on to a path, just past the end of the woods. Follow the path to another road. Chelsworth Hall can be seen on your left during this section of the walk. Turn left along the road to reach a T-junction. A diversion of about 500 yards turns left here and follows the lane down to the Peacock Inn at **Chelsworth**.

To continue the walk, turn right at the T-junction. Now, just opposite a house and pond on your right, turn left down a waymarked path between hedgerows. The path soon follows the left-hand edge of a field and then goes into woodland. At the end of the woods, go down to a stile and cross it into open access land. From here the route diverts from the right of way and heads towards Nedging Mill, slightly to your right, going past a small sluice. Go to the left of the mill to reach a lane. Turn left, but after about 200 yards, turn left again over a stile and walk down to a bridge over a stream. Turn right, over the bridge, and follow the edge of the stream all the way to a road bridge. Turn right over the bridge to reach a T-junction. Turn left and follow the road back to Bildeston and the Market Square.

POINTS OF INTEREST:

Church of Saint Mary Magdalene, Bildeston – On the south side of the church is the memorial to Captain Edward Rotheram who commanded the *Royal Sovereign*, the lead ship at the Battle of Trafalgar in 1805. He died at Bildeston House in 1830.

Chelsworth – The village is noted for its thatched cottages and Norman Church.

REFRESHMENTS:

The Peacock Inn, Chelsworth.

There are also possibilities in Bildeston.

Maps: OS Sheets Landranger 155; Pathfinder 984.
A circular walk linking Thurston and Pakenham.
Start: At 920652, the car park at New Green Community Centre,
Thurston.

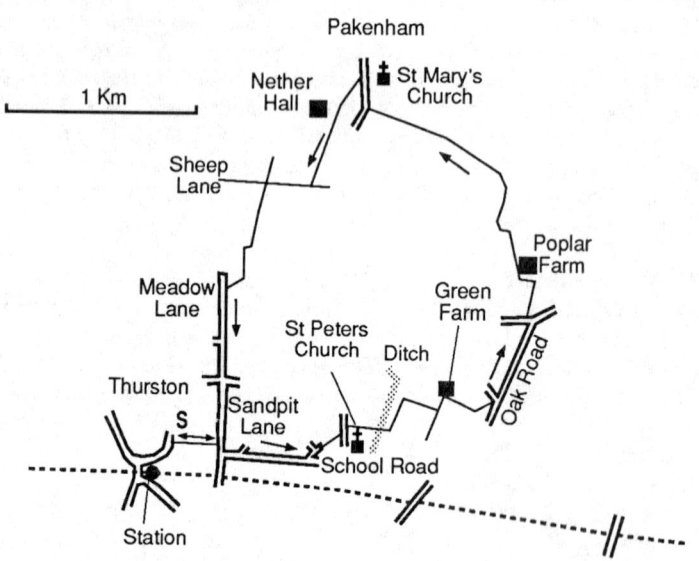

From the car park, follow the tarmaced path from the main road (Station Hill), heading
eastwards between houses and the new Community Centre in **Thurston**. Cross Sandpit
Lane and go along School Road. Now, just before you reach the Primary School, turn
left, passing the school on the right, and go along a tarmaced path to reach Church
Road, with **St Peters Church** opposite. Turn left, and then right to go along the left-
hand side of the church. Follow the path down to a ditch and go left to reach a sleeper
bridge. Cross and continue along the right-hand side of ditch. Go right at the end of
the ditch to reach Green Farm. Follow the path past the farm, continuing along it to
reach Oak Road.

Turn left and follow the road down to a T-junction. Turn left, and then right towards Poplar Farm. Just before reaching a flint wall and barn, turn left to go along to the left-hand side of the barn. Now follow the path diagonally left across a pasture, continuing along it to reach the corner of an orchard. Go to the right-hand side of the orchard heading towards St Mary's Church, Pakenham in the distance. When you reach Pakenham Road, turn right and then left opposite St Mary's Church to go down a pleasant green lane towards Nether Hall. Go past the entrance to the Hall, on your right, and out into a pasture. Cross the pasture to reach a stile. Go over and turn right along Sheep Lane. Just past a bricked entrance to Nether Hall on your right, turn left along a path which leads on to Meadow Lane. Follow Meadow Lane past houses, on your right, to reach its junction with Norton Road. Cross and go down Sandpits Lane to its junction with School Road. Now turn right along a tarmaced path back to the car park.

POINTS OF INTEREST:
Thurston – The village lies on the line of the Roman Road from Long Melford to the 1st-century fort at Pakenham. The village has grown a lot in the recent years and now has a population of some 3000 people. The village hall, known as Cavendish Hall, was given to Thurston in 1912 in memory of William Tyrrell Cavendish, one of the passengers on the ill-fated *Titanic*.
St Peter's Church – The church dates from 1861-2 and replaced a medieval church after its tower collapsed.

REFRESHMENTS:
There are good opportunities in Thurston.

Walk 24   **GRUNDISBURGH**   4m (6½km)

Maps: OS Sheets Landranger 156 and 169; Pathfinder 1008.
A circular walk centred on Grundisburgh.
Start: At 222503, the playing field car park next to the village
hall, Grundisburgh.

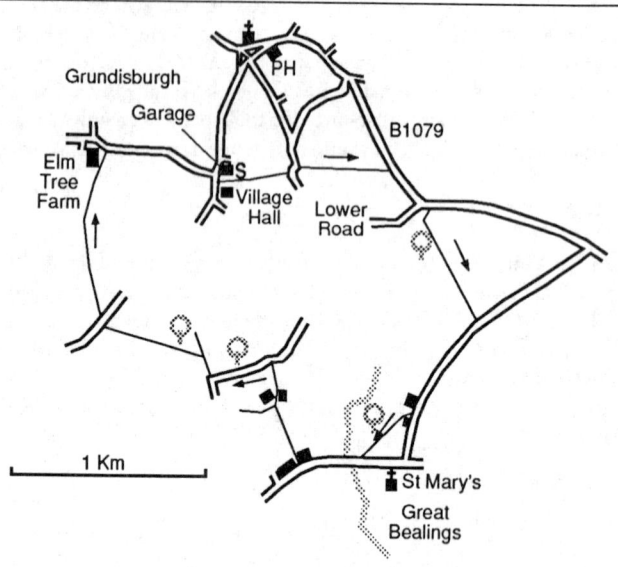

From the car park, head to the left-hand side of the village hall, passing to the left of
the tennis courts. The path now passes behind a shed and continues into a small field.
Take the footpath in the left-hand corner, following it with the back of the houses, on
your left, and an open field on your right. Continue along the path to reach a road (the
B1079). Turn right, with care, and follow the road, passing Bridge House, to reach a
road on your right (Lower Road). Continue along the main road for a further 100 yards,
then, where the road bears to the left, take a waymarked path on the right, going
around the right-hand edge of a field. The path soon turns to the left and passes between
fields, becoming a sandy track. Continue along this track to reach the top of a hill.
Now follow the track down the left-hand side of an open field to reach a metalled
lane.

Turn right and follow the lane past a gas installation on the left. After a further 500 yards, take a waymarked path on the right, going between houses to reach a stile into a paddock. Cross the stile and turn left to head for another stile in the fence. Cross, turn right, and then immediately left to go behind some trees, following a path down a slope to reach a pasture. Continue in approximately the same direction, heading towards a stile on to a metalled lane to the left of a bridge. From here you can take a short detour along the path opposite to visit **Great Bealings Church**.

The route turns right and follows the lane over the bridge and past the old vicarage. About 200 yards beyond the bridge, take a waymarked path on the right, following it between houses and across an open field, heading towards poplar trees in the distance. Maintain direction past the trees and go uphill to reach a track on a corner. Turn right along the track, passing a house on the right and continuing to reach a metalled lane. Turn left and follow the lane, with woods on your right, until it turns sharp left. There, turn right through a gate to follow the track beyond, with the woods still on your right.

Soon you will reach an open field: follow the left-hand hedge and, after some 50 yards, turn left to go through the hedge. Now follow a waymarked path, with woodland again on your right. The path soon takes you down the left-hand side of a field to reach a metalled lane. Turn right, passing a house on your left, and then turn left along a waymarked path, following it around the left-hand side of a field. Continue along the path until just before Elm Tree Farm, where the path bears right and over a stile into a pasture. Cross this and another stile on to a metalled lane. Turn right and follow the lane down to a T-junction. Turn right, and then left, just past the Texaco garage, to return to the playing field car park.

POINTS OF INTEREST:

St Mary's Church, Great Bealings – This fine church is noted for its wood carvings and its porch, built in memory of Sir Thomas Seckford of Seckford Hall who founded Woodbridge School.

REFRESHMENTS:
The Dog, Grundisburgh.

Walk 25   THORNHAM MAGNA   4m (6¹/₂km)

Maps: OS Sheets Landranger 156; Pathfinder 964.

A walk around the Thornham Estate.

Start: At 108715, the Field Studies Centre car park, Thornham Magna.

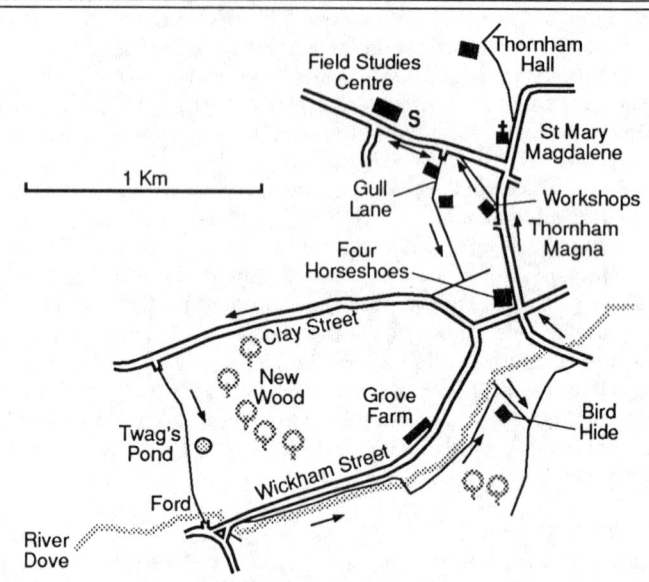

From the **Thornham Estate** Field Studies Centre car park, go out of the main entrance, cross the road and turn left to follow a path down the right-hand side of the road. At the path's junction with a track, turn right to go along the track (Gull Lane), passing a thatched cottage on your right. At the end of the lane, keep straight on, passing another thatched cottage, on your left, and crossing a bridge into a field. Keep straight on, walking along a line of cherry trees. At the end of the field, go across a ditch and turn right, keeping to the right-hand side of a plantation (Lock's Wood).

Soon, go over another ditch to reach a metalled road (Clay Street). Turn right and follow Clay Street for some ³/₄ mile, then, just past some cottages on the right, turn left down a track. Follow the track past two ponds on your left **(Twag's Pond)**, and then cross the River Dove by means of a ford to reach a main road. Turn left, cross a bridge and then go right, over a stile and follow the bank of the river. Continue beside the river until you reach another stile. Cross the stile and then the river by way of a concrete and iron bridge. Now follow the other bank of the river to reach a stile near a bird hide. Do not cross the stile: instead, turn right, passing the bird hide. At the top of the hill turn left into a green lane.

Follow the lane until you reach Water Lane Cottage. There, cross the river by a bridge or ford and continue along the lane back towards Thornham Magna to reach a crossroads. Go straight over, passing the Four Horseshoes on your left, following The Street. The small cottage on the left used to be the Thornham Reading Rooms.

Just beyond the Street Forge Workshops, take the path on the left, following it to return to the top of Gull Lane. Now reverse the outward journey to return to the car park.

POINTS OF INTEREST:

Thornham Estate – The estate has been owned by the Henniker family since 1756. The present Lord and Lady Henniker opened up the estate for educational and recreational purposes and to provide local employment. The estate now combines a working farm, with forestry, shooting and workshops. There are also several circular walks and a Field Studies Centre.

Twag's Pond – These ponds are typical of Suffolk farm ponds once used to provide drinking water for livestock. Since farms are no longer dependent on natural water supplies, a lot of the ponds have been neglected and have silted up. In 1992, Twag's Pond was cleaned out and re-profiled in order to provide a better habitat for frogs, toads and newts, these amphibians spending much of their time on the margins of a pond. The surrounding scrub is also coppiced on a regular basis so as not to shade out the pond too much.

REFRESHMENTS:

The Four Horseshoes, Thornham Magna.

There is also a tea rooms beside the car park at the start/finish of the walk.

Walk 26   HOLBROOK AND ALTON WATER   4m (6¹/₂km)

Maps: OS Sheets Landranger 169; Pathfinder 1053.

A circular walk beside the River Stour and Alton Water.

Start: At 177351, the car park at Lower Holbrook.

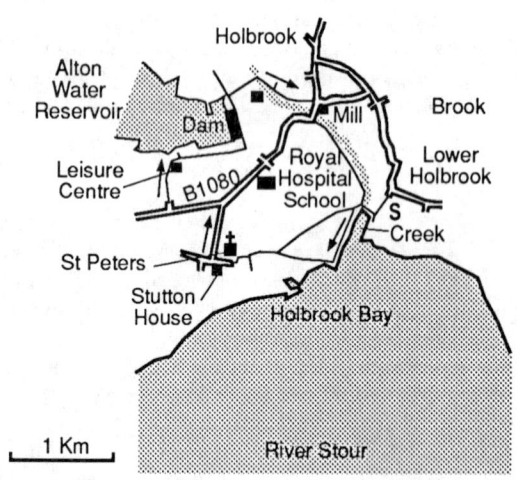

From the car park, go through the kissing gate and along the wide track to Holbrook Creek. Here the track divides: take the right-hand branch that runs beside the river wall. Soon the track turns to the left and passes a boat yard: turn left just after the boat yard and follow a path along the top of the river wall. To the right you get a very fine view of the **Royal Hospital School**.

At the end of the wall (after about 1,000 yards) turn right, down some steps and go across a bridge into an open field. Follow the right-hand edge of the field until you come to a track on the left, with a hedgerow either side. Follow the track past a club house, on the right, and a house, on the left. Where the track turns sharp left, keep straight on along a path, crossing open grassland. At the top of a slight hill, the path turns left, and then, soon, right, becoming a lane as it passes St Peter's Church, on the right, and **Stutton House**, on the left.

Follow the lane to its junction with a road. Turn right and follow the road to a T-junction with the B1080. Turn left, with care, and follow this main road for some 500 yards to reach the entrance to **Alton Water Reservoir**, on your right.

Turn right and follow the road into the reservoir area, passing the Visitor's Centre, on your right, and, beyond, the Sports Centre, on your left. Continue along the road and then turn left to cross the top of the dam. At the far side of the dam, go across the bridge over the outfall, through a gate and then turn right to follow a path between two fences, with the treatment works on your right.

Follow the path downhill and around to the right. At this point the waymarked path goes off to the left: ignore this path, keeping straight on, following a small brook, firstly with it on your left, and then on your right. Follow the path through a plantation to reach the main road (the B1080) again. Turn right and walk past **Holbrook Mill**. Just beyond the mill, on a sharp corner of the main road, next to a disused shop, turn left along a track signposted for Lower Holbrook. Follow the track to reach a path leading off to the right. Continue along this delightful path, with the mill brook on your left, for about 1,000 yards to rejoin the main track by the marina. Turn left along the track, with the river wall on your right, soon bearing left to return to the car park.

POINTS OF INTEREST:
Royal Hospital School – The school, for the sons of officers and men in the Royal Navy and Royal Marines, was transferred from Greenwich in 1933.
Stutton House – This was one of the six local manor houses mentioned in the Doomsday book.
Alton Water Reservoir – The reservoir was created in 1973 and supplies drinking water to much of South-East Suffolk. It receives its supply via an underground pipe from the River Gipping at Sproughton. It also provides leisure facilities in the form of sailing, windsurfing and sub-aqua, as well as providing circular walks and a cycle track.
Holbrook Mill – There has been a mill on this site since 1657. The mill ceased working earlier this century and has been converted into a restaurant.

REFRESHMENTS:
The Compasses, Holbrook.
Refreshments are also available at the Alton Reservoir complex.

Walk 27   **DEBENHAM**   4m (6¹/₂km)

Maps: OS Sheets Landranger 156; Pathfinder 985.

Along green lanes from the village.

Start: At 175631, the car park by Barclays Bank, Debenham.

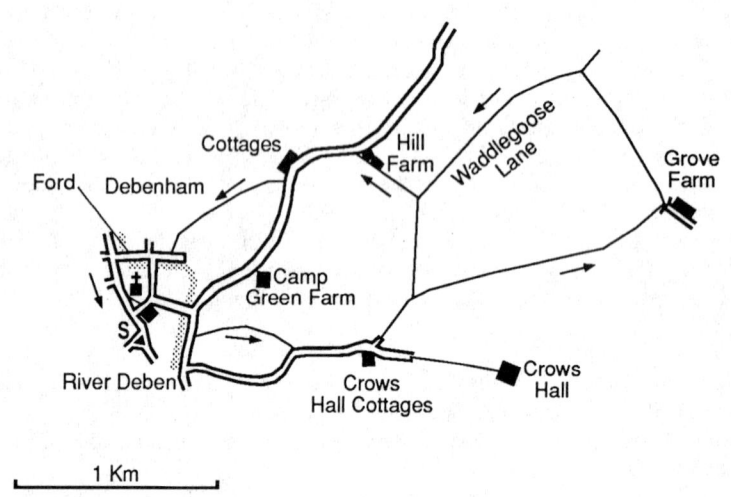

Please note: this walk can be very muddy in wet weather.

From the car park, turn left and follow the lane down to a bridge over the River Deben. Cross and continue to a road junction. Turn right, but after some 100 yards, take the footpath on the left, going uphill with open fields to your left and right. Go over a stile and follow the left-hand edge of a field beyond around to a metalled lane. Turn left, but after some 400 yards, opposite some cottages on the right (Crows Hall Cottages), turn left again, on to a bridleway.

Follow the bridleway for 1 mile to reach its junction with another track at Grove Farm. Turn left and follow the track for some 800 yards to reach a track junction. Turn left, heading down towards Debenham. Continue along this green lane (Waddlegoose Lane) for a further 1,000 yards to reach a junction of tracks. Turn right, following a track past Hill Farm, and continuing to reach a metalled lane. Turn left, following the lane past some cottages on the right. Just beyond the last cottage and barn, turn right along a waymarked path, following the right-hand edge of a field.

The path soon goes downhill, passing allotments, on your right, and continuing to reach a metalled lane (Priory Lane). Bear right and follow the lane to a ford close to the source of the River Deben. Unfortunately nowadays, the river is often dry here. Continue along the lane to its junction with the High Street. Turn left and, at the top of the hill, turn left again into the churchyard of St Mary's Church, **Debenham**. Bear right through the churchyard and go out to reach Cross Green and the end of the walk.

POINTS OF INTEREST:

Debenham – Debenham is a delightful village with many timbered buildings that are typical of wool towns in the area. It lies at the source of the River Deben that reaches the North Sea at Felixstowe.

Many people will recognise the village name as that of a chain of high street stores. The founder of the stores grew up in Debenham, naming them after the village.

REFRESHMENTS:

There are several possibilities in the village of Debenham.

Walk 28　　　**GREAT FINBOROUGH**　　　4m (6¹/₂km)

Maps: OS Sheets Landranger 155; Pathfinder 1007.
A walk through Stowmarket Golf Course.
Start: At 014577, street parking in Great Finborough.

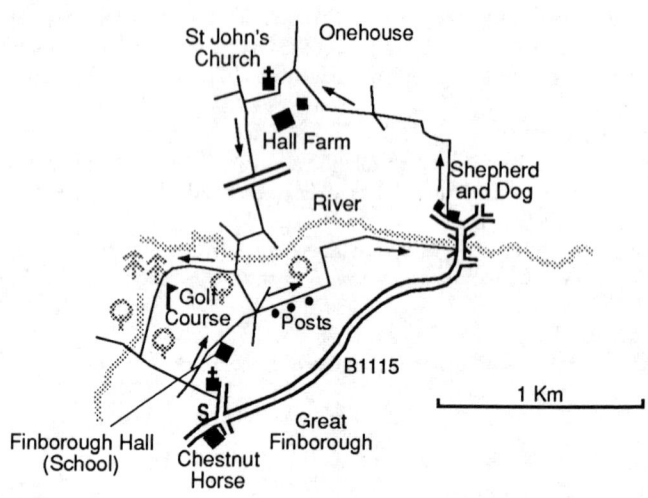

Walk up the lane to St Andrew's Church and take the footpath on its left-hand side.
Go over a stile and turn right to follow the right-hand edge of an arable field behind
the church. At the corner of the field, pass through the hedge on to Stowmarket Golf
Course. The route across the golf course is ill-defined, but does avoid crossing the
fairways: follow the right-hand edge of the grass behind the school to soon reach a
metalled track and waymarker. Cross the track and follow the line of posts on the
right-hand side of a fairway. Maintain direction to the end of the golf course and bear
left there, towards a stile and waymarker next to a hedge. Go over the stile and turn
sharp left to go around the edge of a field to reach a wooden bridge. Cross the bridge
and follow the bank of the river to reach a bridge and a road (the B1115).

Cross the bridge, with care, and take the first turning on the left to reach the Shepherd and Dog. Just beyond the public house, take the footpath on the right, following it into a field behind some houses. Follow the right-hand edge of the field to the corner, and there turn left to continue along the field edge, ignoring a waymarker pointing to a path on the right. After a sharp turn to the right, take a waymarked cross-field path on the left, crossing to the far field corner. Now keep straight on, heading for Hall Farm in the distance and walking with a hedgerow on your right. At the end of the hedge, just before a barn, turn right into the adjacent field and follow its left-hand edge. After some 300 yards, turn left to reach the corner of a gravel track. Keep straight on along this track towards **St John the Baptist Church**, Onehouse. Bear left in front of the church and follow a track into an open field. After 100 yards, turn left along a waymarked path, with a hedgerow on your right and a wire fence on your left. Maintain direction to reach a metalled lane.

Cross the lane and follow the path opposite, going down the left-hand side of a wood. Soon the path meets a track: turn right to reach, after a few yards, a track junction. Turn left and follow the track to a bridge. Cross the bridge, returning to the golf course. Turn right and head towards a group of trees. Just before a group of conifers on the left, turn left and follow the left-hand side of a fairway. At the end of the fairway, continue along a path through the woods. On reaching a junction of paths with a bridge on the right, turn left to reach an open field. Turn left again to follow a path back to St Andrew's Church. Turn right along the metalled lane and back to the centre of **Great Finborough**.

POINTS OF INTEREST:

Great Finborough – Finborough Hall, now a boarding school, was the manor house for the Finborough Estate. The estate was sold off in 1935 to pay death duties.
St John the Baptist Church – The church pre-dates the Norman Conquest, having an Anglo-Saxon round tower, but an Elizabethan porch.

REFRESHMENTS:
The Chestnut Horse, Great Finborough.
The Shepherd and Dog, Onehouse.

Walk 29   **WALPOLE**   4m (6¹/₂km)

Maps: OS Sheets Landranger 156; Pathfinder 965.

An interesting circular walk from the village.

Start: At 365745, the centre of the village of Walpole.

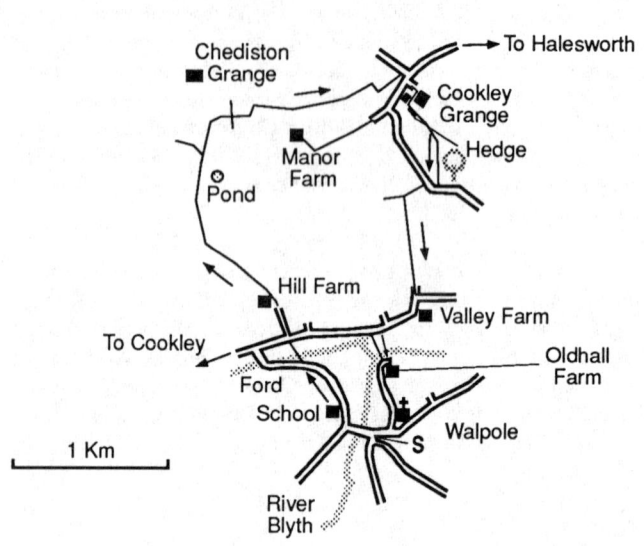

Leave the village by the Heveningham road (the B1117) and cross the bridge over River Blyth. After a few yards, bear right along a metalled lane, soon passing the Cookley and Walpole Primary School on your left. Ignore the first footpath on the right, but take the second, crossing a meadow and then a bridge, and continuing to reach a metalled lane at a T-junction. Cross the lane and continue straight on, going along the driveway to Hill Farm. Go to the right of the farmhouse to continue along a driveway, going uphill with large, open fields to both your left and right.

Go past a pond, on your right, and then, where the track turns left, keep straight on along another track. Soon this track bears to the right: walk to the end of the field and then go through the hedge, continuing with a hedgerow on your right. At the end of the next field, turn left, and then right, by a waymarker, into another field. Now walk with the hedgerow on your left, going through several fields to reach a metalled lane. Turn right, soon reaching a road junction. Now follow the driveway opposite to reach Cookley Grange.

At the farm, turn right in front of the farmhouse, and then left at its end to follow the hedge on your right. Follow the hedge into an open arable field, and there bear slightly right to go along a cross-field path towards a line of trees. Continue along the path to reach a sleeper bridge, crossing it to reach a metalled lane. Turn right, but after a few yards turn left along a gravel trackway. After about 200 yards you will reach a junction of tracks: turn left and follow the track to reach a metalled lane. Keep straight on, along the lane, passing Valley Farm House on your left. Continue for another 400 yards and then, just before a wood on your left, turn left through a metal gate. Bear slightly left and cross the field beyond, heading towards a distant farmhouse. Cross a bridge on the far side of the field and then head for a gate on the left. Go through and turn right along a metalled lane towards **Walpole**, passing St Mary's Church on your left. At the road junction with the B1117, turn right, with care, and follow the road to the start of the walk.

POINTS OF INTEREST:
Walpole – The village boasts the oldest chapel in East Anglia. Originally built in 1607 its was adapted as a chapel in 1647 and enlarged some time before 1698. The original mullion windows still survive.

REFRESHMENTS:
None in Walpole or en route, the nearest being in Halesworth, to the north-east along the B1117, or in Huntingfield, to the south-west, just off the B1117.

Maps: OS Sheets Landranger 155; Pathfinder 984.
A fine walk past Rougham Church.
Start: At 917618, the lay-by opposite the Bennet Arms, Rougham.

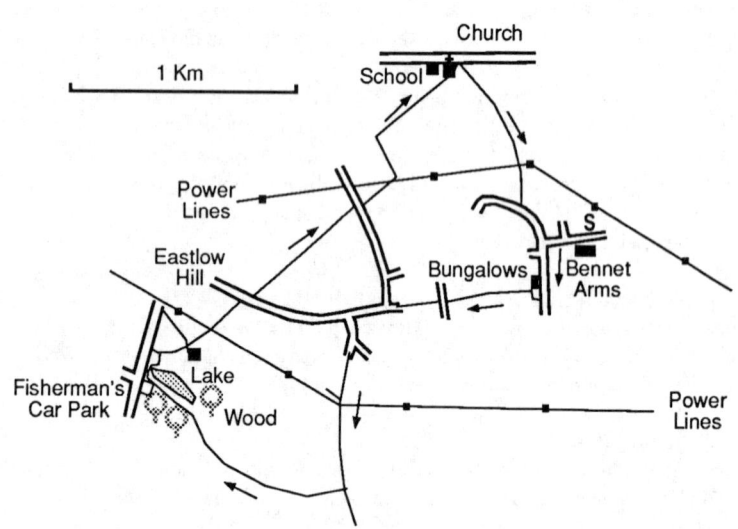

From the lay-by, walk past the **Bennet Arms** towards the village. At the T-junction, turn left, soon passing the Post Office on your left. Now, just past some bungalows on your right, turn right up a waymarked path. Follow the path behind the end bungalow and across an arable field. At the far side of the field you will reach a track: turn left, then right to go along another track, following it to the corner of a metalled lane. Carry straight along the lane, but after 250 yards, turn left along another lane signposted to Green Farm.

Where the lane bears left, continue straight on along a green track, and where this track turns sharp right, keep straight on again, following the left-hand side of a field. At the bottom of the field, cross a sleeper bridge and turn sharp right to follow the edge of a large arable field, with a hedgerow and ditch on your right. Maintain direction, following the right-hand field edges as you cross several sleeper bridges and reach the edge of a wood. Cross yet another sleeper bridge and follow the path through the wood maintaining direction at all times. Soon you come to the end of a fishing lake: turn left to follow a path along the side of the lake.

At the far end of the lake you will reach a car park: turn right around the end of the lake. The path soon becomes indistinct but a little further on you will reach a chestnut fence. Turn right and follow a path to a stile. Cross the stile and, after a few yards, cross a second stile to reach a lawn. Maintain direction with a hedge on your left, soon crossing a driveway and continuing to reach another stile. Cross the stile into the adjacent field and maintain direction to reach a stile on the far side. Again maintain direction, crossing the next field heading to the right of an oak tree to reach a stile. Cross on to a metalled lane (Eastlow Hill).

Turn right, but after a few yards turn left over a stile into a pasture. Bear right and head for a gate. Go through and maintain direction to reach a second gate. Go through and bear left across the pasture beyond to reach a stile in the far corner. Cross and go down the left-hand side of the field beyond to reach a metalled lane. Cross the lane and follow the right-hand edge of the field opposite to reach its far end. Go through the hedge and turn sharp left down the left-hand side of the next field. Again go through the hedge, but this time turn sharp right and follow the right-hand side of the field. Soon you will climb a small hill: go across a school playing field and into a churchyard. Pass to the left of the church to reach a road. Turn right and, within a few yards, turn right again to follow the path back to **Rougham**. Where the path meets a metalled lane, turn left and follow the lane around a corner to reach a T-junction. Turn left and follow the lane back past the Bennet Arms and the end of the walk.

POINTS OF INTEREST:

Bennet Arms – The public house gets its name from one of the residents of Rougham Hall. The hall was bombed in World War II and not rebuilt.

Rougham – The original village of Rougham was centred on the church, but as a result of plague the houses were burnt down and rebuilt in the surrounding area.

REFRESHMENTS:

The Bennet Arms, Rougham.

Walk 31　　　**ALDRINGHAM**　　　4m (6$\frac{1}{2}$km)

Maps: OS Sheets Landranger 156; Pathfinder 987.

A circular walk across heathland and along a disused railway.
Start: At 445610, the car park by the Parrot and Punchbowl,
Aldringham.

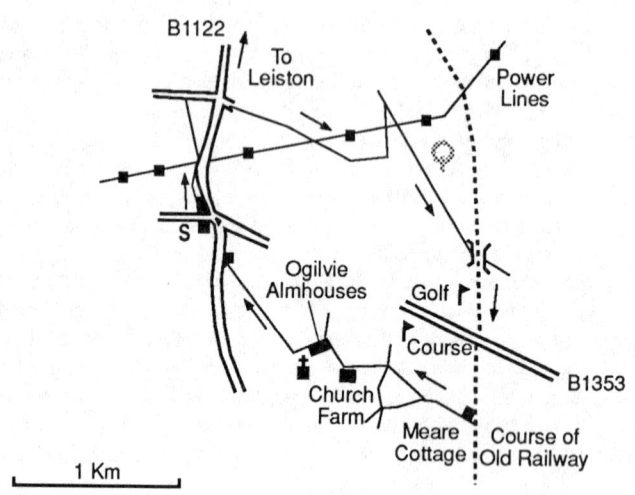

From the car park, take the path to the left of the **Craft Market** and follow it until just
before it meets the Leiston Road. There, bear left and follow a cross-field path,
continuing to reach a metalled lane. Turn right and follow the lane to reach the Leiston
road (the B1122). Cross the road and go down the turning opposite, soon reaching a
footpath on the left. Follow this path along the right-hand side of a large arable field,
heading slightly uphill, with a view of the Sizewell A and B nuclear power stations on
your left. The stations explain the power lines that cross the route.

At the top of the hill you will reach the end of some hedgerows: pass between
hedges initially, and then turn sharp left to follow the left-hand edge of an adjacent
field. The path soon joins another footpath: turn right to head back in the direction
you have just come. Continue along this path, maintaining direction across a golf

course and then going down to the remains of a railway bridge. Go 'under' the bridge, and then turn sharp right to follow the course of the **old railway**. Follow the path of the railway, a nearly straight line, to reach the main road to Thorpeness (the B1353).

Cross the road and follow the track opposite, soon reaching a large barn. There, bear right and follow a smaller path, soon passing down the left-hand side of Meare Cottage. Turn right in front of the cottage, cross the course of the railway and follow the path opposite, going over a wooden bridge. Now continue towards a house on the left. Just before the house, cross the stile on the right and turn sharp left to follow a cross-field path to another stile. Cross this stile and follow the track beyond down to Church Farm. Bear to the right of the farm and follow the track up to the Ogilvie Almshouses.

Turn left to go in front of the almshouses, continuing down to a small church. Now take the path to the right of the church, going downhill. At the bottom of the hill, turn right and follow a path to reach the main Leiston road again. Turn right and follow the road back to the Parrot and Punchbowl.

POINTS OF INTEREST:

Craft Market – The Aldringham Craft Market at the start/end of the walk is well worth a visit.

Old railway – The disused railway line was once the Saxmundham to Aldeburgh branch of the East Suffolk Railway. Built in 1859, the branch line was never successful and after a chequered history it finally closed to passenger traffic in 1961.

REFRESHMENTS:

The Parrot and Punchbowl, Aldringham.

Maps: OS Sheets Landranger 156; Pathfinder 946.
A walk through ancient woodland and along green lanes.
Start: At 488883, the car park next to the Village Hall, Mutford.

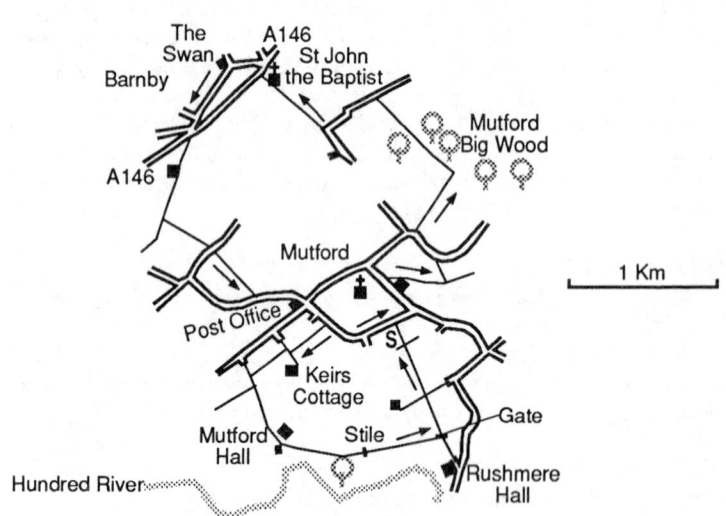

Leave the car park, turn right and walk to the end of Mill Lane. Turn left and, after
300 yards, turn right along a footpath on the right. When you reach an arable field, go
along the left-hand side for a few yards, then go through a gap in the hedge and
continue along the right-hand edge to reach a stile. Cross and turn left to follow a path
to a road. Turn left and follow the road to the next bend, turning right there along a
path heading towards **Mutford Big Wood**. Go across a field to reach the wood and
turn left to follow the edge of the field, with the wood on your right. At the corner of
the field, follow the path into the wood. Follow the path through the wood and, where
it leaves the wood, turn right to follow the edge of an arable field to a metalled road.
Turn left and follow the road for some 400 yards to where it turns sharp left. Turn
right here and follow the path heading towards St John the Baptist Church, Barnby.

On reaching the church, walk around to the front to reach the main Beccles to Lowestoft road (the A146). Cross the road, with care, and go along Swan Lane to reach the Swan. Turn left and continue along the road to reach a junction. Turn left to meet the main road (the A146) again. Cross, again with care, and continue along the track opposite, soon passing a cottage on the right. After a further 400 yards, turn left along a path, following it to a metalled lane (Dairy Lane). Turn right and then, after a few yards, turn left to go down a path, with hedgerow on your left and an open field on your right. Soon you will reach another metalled lane (Beccles Road): turn left and follow the lane to a crossroads. Cross into Mill Lane opposite.

The shorter walk continues along Mill Lane, following it back to the start at Mutford Village Hall.

The longer walk follows Mill Lane, but then turns right along a track just past the end of the cottages on your left. Go along the track to reach a stile. Go over the stile and bear slightly right, crossing two further stiles to reach a track going to Keirs Cottage, on the left. Go straight on, following the hedge on your left to reach a metalled lane. Turn left and follow the lane to Mutford Hall. Pass in front of the Hall, and then bear left, going through a yard and crossing a stile into a pasture. Turn left to follow the edge of the pasture, passing a cottage on the left and continuing to reach a stile, also on the left. Go over the stile and follow the path beyond up a bank and along the left-hand side of a field. Continue along the path though a small wood to reach a stile into a meadow. Cross and turn left to follow the left-hand edge of the meadow. At the end of the meadow, follow a track, with Rushmere Hall on the right. Where the track turns sharp right, turn left to go through a gate and follow the left-hand edge of the field beyond. Cross a track and follow a cross-field path down to a wooden bridge. Cross the bridge and maintain direction to reach a driveway. Cross the driveway and continue along the path to reach Mill Lane. Turn left to return to the Village Hall in **Mutford**.

POINTS OF INTEREST:
Mutford Big Wood – The wood is an ancient woodland which used to supply timber for the building of fishing boats at Lowestoft.
Mutford – St Andrew's Church overwhelms the village. With its lovely restored round tower and Galilee porch, it is well worth a visit.

REFRESHMENTS:
The Swan, Barnby.
Food and drink can also be obtained at the village stores in Mutford.

Walk 34   **ERISWELL**   4m (6½km)

Maps: OS Sheets Landranger 143; Pathfinder 962.

A pleasant walk through forest and heath.

Start: At 723780, St Laurence and St Peter's Church, Eriswell.

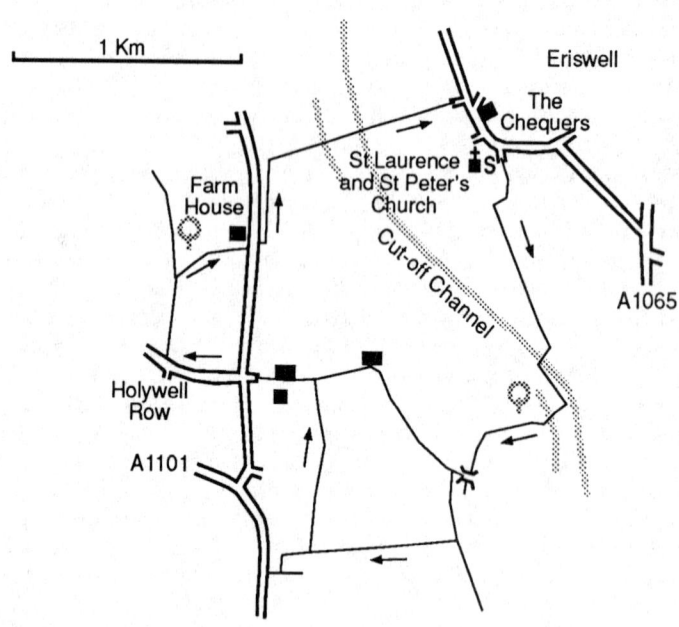

To start the walk, take the track along the left-hand side of St Laurence's Church, **Eriswell**. Soon the track turns right and then, within a few yards turns left: continue along it to reach a bridge over the **Cut-off Channel**. Cross the bridge and turn left, follow the channel's bank (with the channel on your left) for some 200 yards. Now take a waymarked path on the right, soon crossing a bridge over a small drain. Beyond, the path reaches an open field. Follow the right-hand edge of the field to its corner and turn left. Soon you will reach a wooden bridge on the right: cross and bear left to follow a path into woodland. When you reach a junction of tracks, turn left and follow a track to reach a second junction and a waymarker.

Turn right down the wide forest ride, now with coniferous woodland to both your left and right. After some 700 yards you will reach another junction of tracks. Turn right and follow the path/track, initially with woodland on your left and then with an open field on that side. At a T-junction of paths, turn left to pass houses, on both your right and left, continuing to reach a main road. Cross the road and follow the lane opposite into the hamlet of Holywell Row.

Just before a bend in the lane, take a waymarked track on your right. Follow the track for some 400 yards to reach a stile on the right. Cross the stile and follow the very indistinct path beyond, using the right-hand side of a distant farm as a marker. Heading for the farm's right side will bring you to a stile on to a road. Cross the stile and the road, and then turn left to follow another waymarked path along the left-hand edge of a field. At the corner of the field, turn right and follow the field edge down to a small bridge over a ditch. Cross and continue in the same direction, soon reaching another bridge over the Cut-off Channel. Cross the channel and maintain direction to reach another road. Turn right, soon passing the Chequers on the left. A few more yards now brings you back to the church and the start of the walk.

POINTS OF INTEREST:

Eriswell – The manor of Eriswell was bought by the New England Company in 1649 and several houses in the village still retain the inscription NEC. The NEC had a policy of bringing the Christian faith to North American Indians and in 1818, as part of an apprenticeship scheme, a 14 year old Indian was brought to Eriswell. Unfortunately he died 2 years later. His memorial can be seen in the churchyard.

Cut-off Channel – The channel was built to control flooding of the River Lark. It joins the River Lark at Barton Mills and allows flood water to flow into the River Ouse at Denver near Kings Lynn.

REFRESHMENTS:

The Chequers, Eriswell.

Maps: OS Sheets Landranger 169; Pathfinder 1031.
A remote walk around saltmarsh and forest.
Start: At 378471, the Boyton Bell, Boyton.

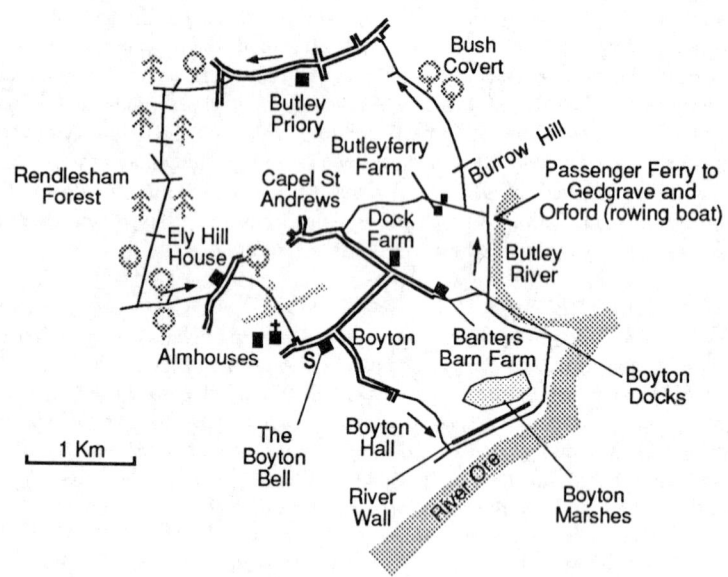

From the Boyton Bell, turn right and, after some 100 yards, turn right again to go
down a lane towards Boyton Hall. Where the lane turns sharp right, keep straight on
along a gravel path to reach the river wall. Turn left and follow the top of the wall,
initially going along the side of the River Ore, and then along the Butley River, to
reach Boyton Dock.

    The shorter walk turns left here, following a track past Banters Barn Farm and
continuing along the farm track to reach its junction with a metalled lane. Turn left
and follow the lane back to the Boyton Bell.

The longer walk continues past Boyton Dock. Continue to a point just before a **ferry jetty.** Now turn left along a waymarked path, heading towards Butley ferry Farm. After some 200 yards, turn right over a stile and up the hill beyond to reach another stile at its top. Cross and maintain direction, going down the other side of the hill to reach the end of a track at a metal gate and stile. Follow the track along the left-hand side of a wood. Now, just past the end of the wood, ignore the first track on the left, but turn left along the second track to go past the cottages at Butley Low Corner. Continue to reach a road junction (Five Cross Ways) at **Butley Priory**. Go along the road opposite, now with Butley Priory Gatehouse on your left, until you come to the end of the wood on your left and a bend in the road. Here, bear left along a gravel track to reach another metalled lane. Cross and follow the track opposite into Rendlesham Forest. Soon you will pass an arable field on your left: continue, now with forest to the left and right. Turn left along the first major ride and follow it for some 500 yards until it crosses another major ride. Keep straight on and, after a further 250 yards, you will reach another ride. Turn left and then, after a few more yards, you will come out to a clearing and a junction of tracks. Bear right and follow the main track for some 600 yards to reach a junction of tracks. Continue straight on for another 700 yards to where the track bends to the right. Here, turn left along a smaller track, following it to a metalled lane. Turn left, passing Ely Hill House, on the left. Now turn right to follow a waymarked path. Cross an arable field, and then follow the left-hand edge until the path bears off to the left through some woodland. Cross a small bridge and then bear right to head for another bridge over the River Tang. Bear slightly right to reach a track and follow it up to the left-hand side of Boyton House. Where you join a driveway, bear left to reach a metalled lane. Turn left and follow the lane back to the Boyton Bell and the end of the walk.

POINTS OF INTEREST:

Ferry Jetty – The Butley ferry service to Gedgrave was introduced by the Austin canons in the 12th century and has recently been revived. To contact the ferryman, telephone Mr Rogers on 01394 410096.

Butley Priory – Founded by Ranulph de Glanville, chief minister to Henry II in 1171, the Priory was destroyed during Henry VIII's Dissolution. Only the gatehouse survived: it was converted into a private home in 1737.

REFRESHMENTS:

The Boyton Bell, Boyton.

Walk 37 NEEDHAM MARKET & PRIESTLEY WOOD 4¹/₂m (7km)
Maps: OS Sheets Landranger 155; Pathfinder 1007.
A walk along green lanes and through ancient woodland.
Start: At 091549, the car park at Needham Market Station.

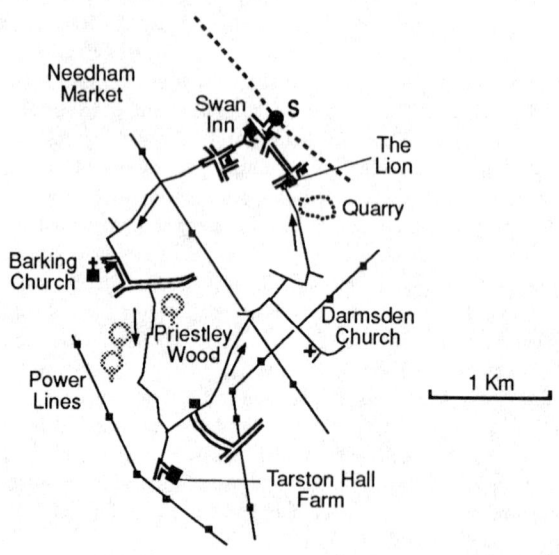

Leave the car park in front of the station, heading along the approach road back to the High Street. Cross the road and head for an alleyway at the side of the Swan Inn. Pass through the car park and go along a bridleway beside the recreation ground (which is on your right). Keep straight on along the track to reach open country. After 500 yards, look out for a small bridge over a ditch on your right. Follow the path over the bridge and immediately turn left along a green lane bordered by hedgerow and trees. Follow this green lane (a causeway) for another 500 yards, eventually reaching a lane leading to **Barking Church**.

Turn left and follow the lane to the main road (the B1078). Turn left along the pavement, then, after about 200 yards, cross, with care, to follow a track into **Priestley Wood**. Continue along this waymarked track, always keeping to the right-hand side of the wood. Eventually you will reach an open field: follow the path along the left-hand side of the field to reach a gap in the hedge on the left. Go through the gap and turn right up a slight hill, again following the edge of the field. Enter the woods at the top of the field and immediately turn left over a small bridge. Now follow the edge of the next field, with a hedge on your left. Maintain direction over another bridge, in the corner of a field, and then go along another hedge to reach the next corner.

Turn left and follow the hedgerow on your right down towards a cottage. The path may not be very distinctive here, but soon a waymarker assists: maintain direction past the cottage, on your left, and along a green lane. Soon the lane opens out on to a track, passing woodland on your right. Where the track turns sharp right towards Darmsden Church, keep straight on along a path across a field. Now turn right, then left, following a path back towards Needham Market passing a quarry on your right. Follow the path to a road and turn right, heading towards the main road. The Lion is to your right here. Turn left at the main road and follow the road back to **Needham Market**. At the Swan Inn (with it on your left), turn right to return to the station car park.

POINTS OF INTEREST:

Barking Church – St Mary's Church is most interesting, with many treasures including a 14th-century chest, a Stuart Holy table, a fine rood screen and a splendid musical instrument called a serpent.

Priestley Wood – This ancient woodland is owned and managed by the Woodland Trust and is noted for its coppicing and associated flora.

Needham Market – This fast growing town has a notable hammerbeam-roofed church and several excellent period houses.

REFRESHMENTS:

The Rampant Horse, Needham.Market
The Swan Inn, Needham.Market
The Lion, Needham.Market

Walk 38   LAVENHAM   4$^{1}/_{2}$m (7km)

Maps: OS Sheets Landranger 155; Pathfinder 1029.

A walk around one of the finest medieval towns in England.

Start: At 914489, the car park at the southern end of the town next to the Cock Inn.

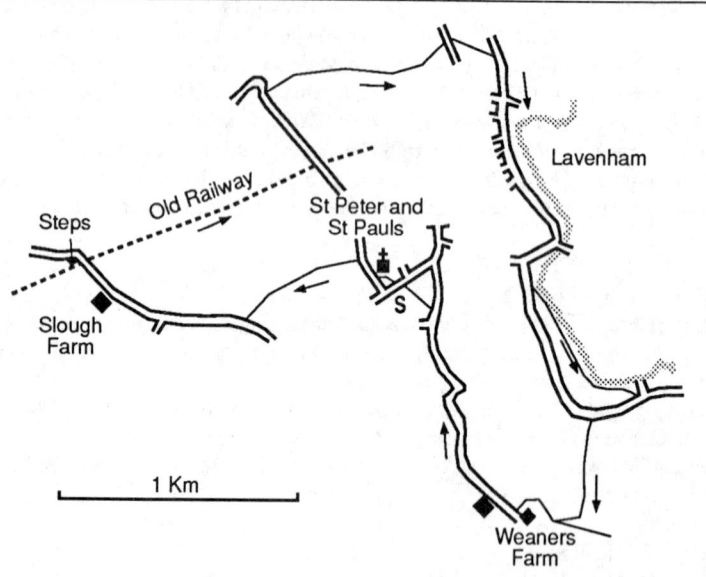

From the car park, cross the main road (the B1071) with care and turn left, and then right, into the **Church of St Peter and St Paul**. Follow the path to the left of the church and then go down to a side lane. Turn right and follow the lane down to a small stream. Turn left and over a couple of stiles. Now follow the path across an open field to reach a lane. Turn right and follow the lane, passing Slough Farm, on the left, to reach the old railway bridge. Just past the bridge, on the left-hand side by a lay-by, follow a path down steps on to the old railway track. Turn left and follow the track which, although muddy at first, soon becomes a pleasant green path later.

After about 900 yards the track meets a metalled lane: turn left and follow the lane for some 500 yards to where a path goes off to the right. Follow this path along the left-hand edge of an open field. Where the path divides, take the left branch, heading towards buildings in the distance. When you reach a road, cross, with care, and follow the path opposite down to Frogs Hall Road. Turn right and cross the old railway bridge, passing the site of the former station on your right. At the main road, cross, with care, and follow the lane down to Brent Eleigh Road.

Turn left, and then immediately left again to follow a path along the edge of a playing field. The path now bears left to follow the river's edge. When you come to the access road to the local sewage works, turn right to reach the main road. Turn right and follow the main road until just before a thatched cottage on the left. Now take a path on the left, heading uphill between the trees. At the top of the hill the path becomes a grassy track: continue along it for some 500 yards and then turn right towards some farm cottages. A diversion on your right takes you around the back of the cottages to meet a lane. Turn right and follow the lane back to **Lavenham**. As you go uphill into the town, there is a path on your left which takes you directly back to the car park.

POINTS OF INTEREST:

St Peter and St Paul Church – The church, at the southern end of Lavenham, was built in the 15th century and has many fine features.

Lavenham – Lavenham is one of the finest medieval towns in England and has a wealth of historical interest that includes over 300 listed buildings. Full information on the town can be found in the Tourist Information Office at the car park entrance.

REFRESHMENTS:

There are ample opportunities in Lavenham.

Walk 39   CRATFIELD $4^1/_2$m (7km)

Maps: OS Sheets Landranger 156; Pathfinder 965.

A circular walk along part of the Roman Road from Peasenhall to Weybread.

Start: At 308751, the car park outside Cratfield village hall.

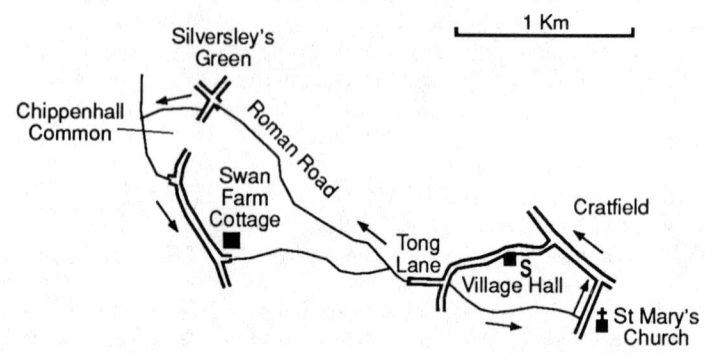

From the car park, turn left, passing the village hall on your left. At the first road junction, turn right along Tong Lane, which starts as a metalled road but soon becomes a muddy track. This lane follows the line of the **Roman Road** from Peasenhall to Weybread. The track eventually reaches a metalled road at Silversley's Green. Turn left but, after a few paces, turn right past a disused house on your right. Once you have come out into an open field, keep straight on across the field to reach **Chippenhall Green**. This common is noted for its traditional grazing and the consequential abundance of wild flowers including the green-winged orchid.

Turn left along the lane, going over the cattle grid and down to a T-junction. Turn right and, just past Swan Farm Cottage on your left, turn left along a rather muddy track. A path at the end of the track passes through a double hedge and then out to join Tong Lane again.

Turn right to retrace your steps back to the road junction. Now take the footpath opposite the junction, going through an orchard and back to St Mary's Church. At the church, turn left to head back into the village, passing the Poacher Inn on your right. Take the next turning on the left (Manse Lane) to return to the village hall and the car park.

POINTS OF INTEREST:

Roman Road – Tong Lane lies on top of part of the Roman Road from Peasenhall to Pulham in Norfolk. Peasenhall was at a junction of roads, one from Coddenham (the site of a Roman Fort) and possibly one from Dunwich although this is only conjecture. The roads were built in the 1st century AD as military routes during the Roman Conquest and represented the first purpose built thoroughfares around Britain. In Suffolk their construction was mainly of local gravel to form the raised bank (agger) with a surface of rammed small stones. Unfortunately once the surface stones are displaced the gravel agger soon deteriorates often leaving little of the road except for a gravely streak across a field or a parch mark in a cereal crop.

Chippenhall Green – This common is still traditionally grazed and as such it has maintained a lot of wildflowers that used to be common throughout East Anglia. It is especially noted for green-winged and bee orchids.

REFRESHMENTS:
The Poacher Inn, Bell Green, Cratfield.

Walk 40   **PAKENHAM** $4^{1}/_{2}$m (7km)

Maps: OS Sheets Landranger 155; Pathfinder 984.

A fine walk passing two working mills.

Start: At 930671, the car park at the rear of St Mary's Church, Pakenham.

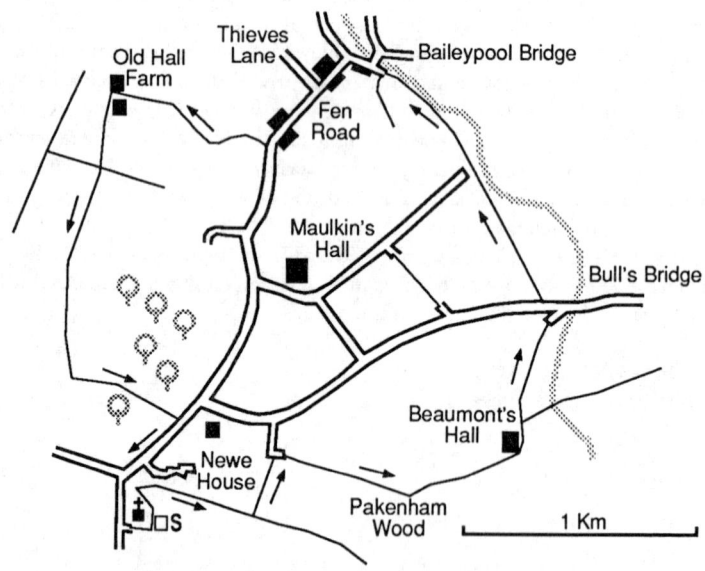

From the car park at the back of **St Mary's Church,** head towards a kissing gate in the fence to the right-hand side of the church. Go down the steps and bear right, going slightly uphill to reach a stile at the top of the field. Cross the stile and turn left, and then right, to cross an open field towards Pakenham Wood. Follow the track into the wood and then, just after the corner of a field on your right, turn left along a track. The track soon joins another at a corner: turn right and follow the edge of Pakenham Wood, on your right. At the end of the wood, bear left towards Beaumont's Hall and then follow the main track down to the road at Bull's Bridge.

76

Cross the road and follow a waymarked path, keeping the river on your right. The path eventually reaches Baileypool Bridge. Bear left to follow the metalled road to its junction with Fen Road. A short detour turns right here, following the road down to **Pakenham Watermill** which is open to the public during the summer.

The route turns left and follows Fen Road passing Thieves Lane on your right. **Pakenham Windmill**, which is open to the public by appointment, is some 1,000 yards along the lane.

Go past Thieves Lane and take the path on the right. Follow the path across a pasture, and then go left and right, heading towards Old Hall Farm seen in the distance. Just beyond the farm, take the path on the left, in front of a pond, and follow it, with a ditch on your left, back towards Pakenham. Cross a stile and turn left to follow the path behind some houses. Now go through a wood to reach a road. Turn right and follow the road past the Post Office, on your right. Now, just before the road junction, take the path on the left, going up a steep hill to return to the church and the starting car park.

POINTS OF INTEREST:

St Mary's Church – This 12th-century church is now more famous for its former rectory, Mulberry House. The rectory had a bricked up window which inspired Rex Whistler, stationed here with the Scots Guards during World War II, to paint a picture of an 18th-century parish priest with wig, gown and candle, writing his sermon. Rex Whistler was killed in action in 1944 and in his memory the window was framed and glazed.

Pakenham Watermill – This 18th-century watermill was restored by the Suffolk Preservation Trust. It is open to the public from 2.00pm – 5.30pm on Wednesdays, Saturdays, Sundays and Bank Holiday Mondays from Good Friday to the end of September.

Pakenham Windmill – This well-known landmark was built in 1816 and restored to full working order in the 1950s. It is open to the public by appointment.

REFRESHMENTS:

The Fox , Pakenham.
The Village Stores and Post Office may also be useful.

Maps: OS Sheets Landranger 155; Pathfinder 984 and 985.

A walk through ancient woods and a wartime airfield.

Start: At 995678, the car park at the rear of All Saints' Church, Great Ashfield.

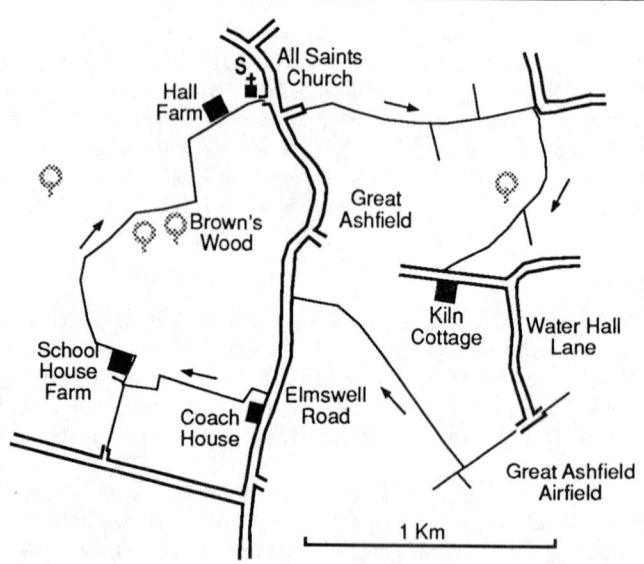

From **All Saints' Church**, turn right and walk along the main road for about 50 yards before turning left up a driveway. The drive soon reaches to a well-defined bridleway leading uphill towards two distant oak trees: continue to the top of the slope and then on to a metalled road, with houses on the right. Turn right to pass along the right-hand side of the first house and then head towards the left-hand side of a small wood. Go over a small bridge and, where a small hedge joins the wood, turn left and head towards the right-hand side of a group of houses, keeping to the edge of the field. The path reaches a metalled road opposite Kiln Cottage: turn left, and then soon right into Water Hall Lane.

Go past Water Hall to reach the old runway of **Great Ashfield Airfield**. Turn right and walk down the concrete runway to reach a barrier. Turn right and follow a waymarked path beside a hedge to reach a metalled road (Elmswell Road). Turn left, passing the Methodist Chapel, and follow the road for some 500 yards to reach the Coach House, on your right. Just before the buildings, turn right and follow a track past a new plantation, on the right. After the bridge, turn left and follow a ditch along the left-hand side of a field. Continue around the field, turning right and going up towards Schoolhouse Farm.

At the top of the field the path turns left, goes over a bridge and then turns right to reach a metalled driveway to the farm: turn right and go through the farm, keeping the farmhouse and a radio mast on your left. The path turns right, around the farm, and then reaches a track and a large open field: turn right along the track, passing the ancient Brown's Wood on your right. Turn right at the end of the wood, continuing along the track. Soon you turn right to go in front of Hall Farm: the track now leads downhill back to All Saints' Church and the car park.

POINTS OF INTEREST:

All Saints' Church – Legend has it that in 903 AD the body of the Saxon King Edmund, killed by the Danes at Hoxne, rested here on the way to Bury St Edmunds and a cross was erected in commemoration in the churchyard. The cross was removed during the reformation and used in the building of a bridge across the stream next to the church. In the 19th century the cross was moved again and now stands in the grounds of Ashfield House.

Great Ashfield Airfield – Great Ashfield was a Home Defence Air Station during the later part of World War I and also the home of the 385th Bomber Group USAF from June 1944 to August 1945 during World War II.

REFRESHMENTS:

None in Great Ashfield or en route. The nearest are at Badwell Ash, a couple of miles to the north.

Maps: OS Sheets Landranger 156; Pathfinder 965.
A walk beside the River Blyth and the Southwold Railway.
Start: At 388775, the Angel Lane North car park, Halesworth.

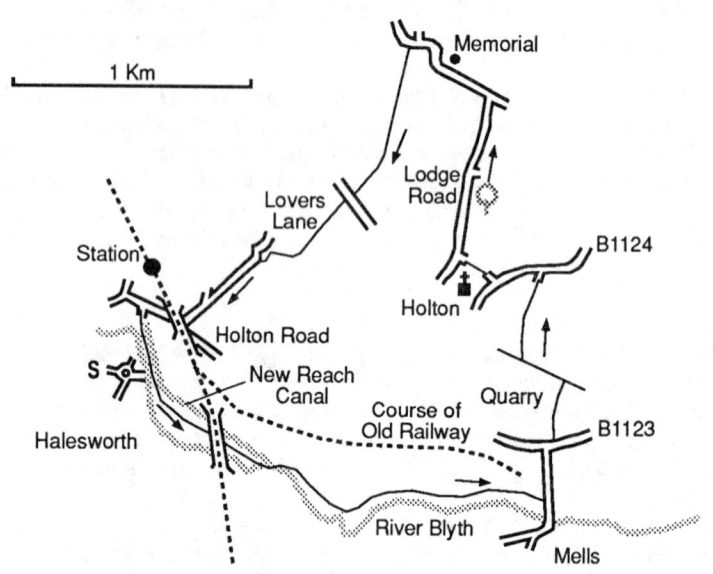

From the car park, cross Saxon Way and go down a waymarked path on the left-hand side of the Old Maltings Leisure Club. Cross the River Blyth and bear right to follow the right-hand bank of 'New Reach' canal. After a short distance a path goes off to the left: follow this to Birds Folly, now a wildlife haven. To continue, keep straight on following the canal, with the railway on your left, to reach a tunnel under the railway. On the other side of the railway, follow the path over the 'New Reach' canal, then turn left to follow the riverbank. When you reach a footbridge, cross and continue along the other riverbank, still heading in the same direction.

    The riverside path passes some fine alder trees before reaching a metalled road at Mells. Turn left and follow the road over the old **Southwold Railway** and up to a T-junction with the Southwold Road (the B1123). Turn right and, after a few yards, turn left – crossing the road with care – to go along a path to the right of some gravel pits. Just past the pits the path meets a main track: turn left passing the pits on the left and after a few yards bear right to follow the track up to the Beccles Road (the B1124). Turn left and, with care, follow the road down into Holton. Now, as you approach St Peter's Church, on the right, take a path also on the right leading past the right-hand side of the church, following it to a metalled road (Lodge Road).

Turn right and follow the road past ancient woodland, on your right, to reach a more major road. Turn left and follow the road for some 400 yards, passing a memorial stone to the 489th Bomb Group USAF, and then turn left down a path going along the right-hand side of an open field. Follow the path to reach a road. Cross and follow the green lane (Lovers Lane) opposite. This green lane soon joins Loam Pit Lane: follow this downhill, passing a cemetery on the left, into Halesworth. At the junction with Holton Road, turn right and go under the railway bridge, noting the remains of the old Southwold Railway bridge abutments. Just after the bridge, turn left by Marlow's Ironmongers, following a path into Town Park. Now follow the riverbank for a short distance before turning right along the path back to the town and car park.

POINTS OF INTEREST:
The Southwold Railway – This three foot gauge railway ran from Halesworth via Wenhaston, Blythburgh and Walberwick to Southwold. It was built in 1878/9 and opened on September 24 1879. It was always in financial difficulties and when the Southwold Corporation allowed motor coaches to operate within its boundaries the fate of the railway was sealed. The last train ran on 11th April 1929 and the trackway was demolished in 1941.

REFRESHMENTS:
There are numerous possibilities in Halesworth, at the start and end of the walk, as well as in Holton along the way.

Walk 43   CLAYDON   4¹/₂m (7km)

Maps: OS Sheets Landranger 155, 156 and 169; Pathfinder 1007.
A pleasant walk around Claydon village.
Start: At 128501, the Claydon picnic site car park.

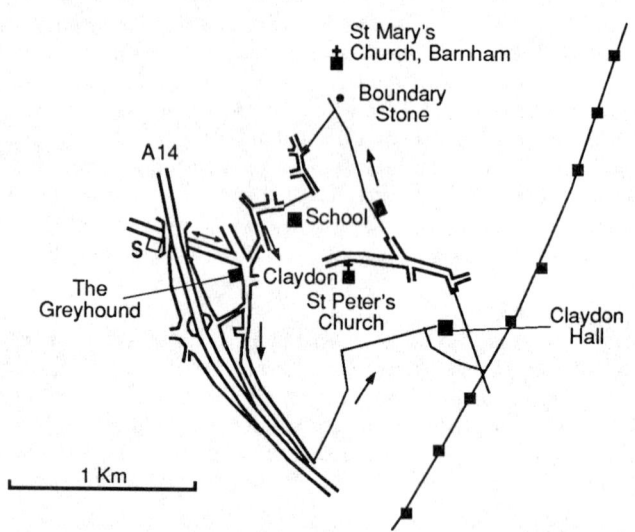

From the car park, turn right to go under the A14 and then follow the road (Station Road) into Claydon. Turn right past the Greyhound and, where the road bears to the right, go straight on along the old Ipswich Road. After about 1,000 yards, you will reach a barrier across the road: turn left along a waymarked track, going up a slight hill. At the top of the hill the track bears left, and then right, towards Claydon Hall. Just before the Hall, turn right along a track leading to a horse paddock. Cross the stile into the paddock and cross to another stile on the left, taking care with the electric fence.

Now maintain direction, passing some small ponds on the left and heading for a stile. Cross the stile and turn left down a bridleway, crossing the entrance to Claydon Hall Farm and continuing down to a metalled road. Turn left and follow the road down to a road junction. At this point you can take a small diversion along the road to your left to visit **St Peter's Church.**

To continue the walk, turn right at the road junction and follow the road past a recreation ground, on the left, to reach a barrier across the now unmetalled track. To the right, close to a gate is an old boundary stone, marking the boundary between Claydon and Barnham parishes.

Retrace your steps for some 100 yards and take the path on your right, going between fields and heading towards a housing estate in the distance. The path becomes tarmaced and leads between bungalows to reach Thornhill Road. Turn left and follow the road to where it ends. There, take the path on the right, following it down past the primary school to reach York Crescent. Turn left and, after some 100 yards, bear right to go down a back lane to reach the Old Ipswich Road opposite the Greyhound. Bear right and then left to go down Station Road, reversing the outward route to return to the car park.

POINTS OF INTEREST:

St Peter's Church – This fine church was declared redundant in 1975 and many of its furnishings were moved to St Mary's Church, Barnham. For some years the church was left to decay until it was taken over by the Church's Conservation Trust who now maintain it. The parish church of St Mary's, Barnham has now been rededicated to St Mary and St Peter.

REFRESHMENTS:

There are no refreshments en route, but there are numerous opportunities in Claydon.

Walk 44   **HINTLESHAM**   4$\frac{1}{2}$m (7km)

Maps: OS Sheets Landranger 169; Pathfinder 1030.

A fine walk around the village of Hintlesham.

Start: At 087434, the car park opposite the Community Hall, Hintlesham.

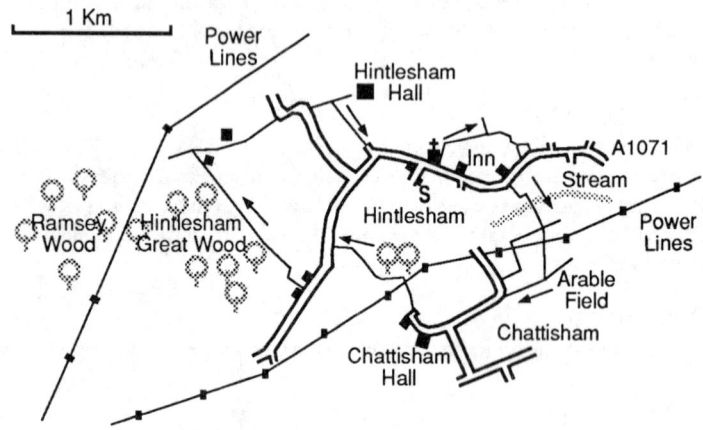

From the car park, walk back to the main road and cross to the church. Turn left down the path between the church and Forge Garage. Go behind the garage and follow the path to the golf course. Continue along the path to reach a track. Turn right and follow the track, with an open field on your right, until you reach a hedgerow, also on your right. Now turn right and follow the path to the main road (the A1071).

Turn right and, after some 100 yards, cross the road to take a path on the left, opposite "South View". Go down this pleasant path with hedgerows on either side, crossing two stiles, and then continuing down to a wooden bridge. Cross the bridge and continue to reach an arable field. Maintain direction for some 400 yards across this field and then turn right along a path, heading down to a metalled lane. Bear left and follow the lane until it turns left at a junction. There, turn right and continue along Chattisham Hall Lane, passing Chattisham Hall on your left. Walk to the end of the lane and then continue along a path with a hedgerow on your left.

At the bottom of the field, turn left and follow the path, with woods on your right, to reach a bridge. Turn right and follow the track up to a metalled lane. Turn left, then, after 100 yards, just past Nutfield Cottage, turn right along a track. The path soon goes along the right-hand side of a field and then passes to the right of Hintlesham Great Wood.

Walk along the edge of the wood, turning left at a bridge to continue along the wood edge. At the end of the wood, bear right to pass some cottages on the right. Now turn right along a track, soon reaching the busy A1071 road. Bear right, with care, to continue along the road to where it bends right. There, carry straight on along the driveway into **Hintlesham Hall**.

Follow the driveway around to the right to return to the main road. Turn left and, again with care, follow the road to St Nicholas' Church, Hintlesham. Now turn right down the driveway to return to the car park.

POINTS OF INTEREST:
Hintlesham Hall – Until 1909, Hintlesham village was part of the Hintlesham Hall estate. The Hall itself, with its Queen Anne front, is now a hotel, its grounds having been turned into a golf course.

REFRESHMENTS:
The George, Hintlesham.

Walk 45   **GREAT GLEMHAM**   4¹/₂m (7km)

Maps: OS Sheets Landranger 156; Pathfinder 986.

A pleasant walk around the village.

Start: At 339616, the lay-by next to All Saints' Church, Great Glemham.

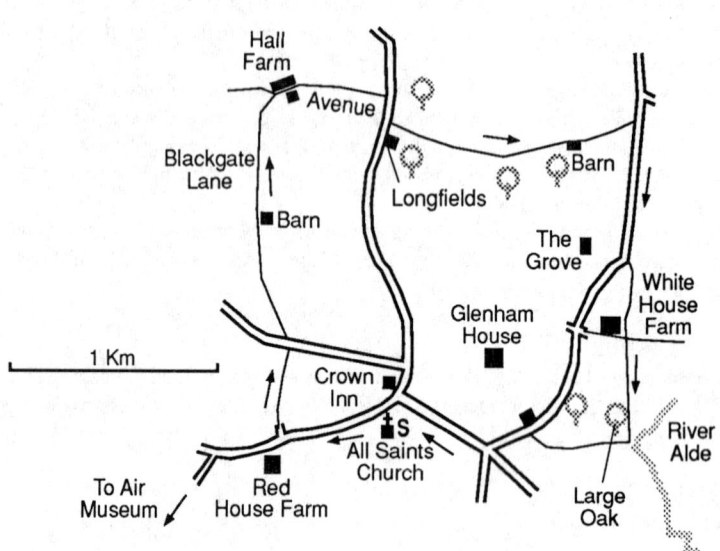

From the lay-by outside the church in **Great Glemham**, turn left and follow the main road from the village for some 500 yards to reach Red House Farm on the left. The road is not very busy and in autumn there is the added bonus of a vast number of blackberries in the hedgerow. Opposite Red House Farm, take the waymarked track, on your right, following it to reach a metalled lane. Turn right and then, within a few paces, turn left up a gravel track (Blackgate Lane). Follow the lane past a barn, on your right, and open fields, on your left, to reach a junction of tracks. Turn right, walk through Hall Farm and continue along the now-metalled lane, with poplar trees to both your right and left. At the end of the lane, turn right and then, after some 100 yards, just before 'Longfields', turn left along a bridleway.

Follow the bridleway past woods on both the left and right to reach a junction of tracks. There, keep straight on along a path, with newly planted trees to your left, and an open field to your right. At the end of the field, go over a sleeper bridge and follow a cross-field path across the next field. At the far side of the field you will join a track: keep straight on down the track, passing a brick barn on your right.

Soon you will reach a metalled lane: turn right and follow the lane for some 600 yards to reach a stile and footpath on your left, just opposite the entrance to 'The Grove'. Follow the path diagonally to the right to reach a stile in the distant fence. Cross the stile and head towards the distant farm buildings to reach a farm gate. Go through the gate and the farmyard to reach a main track. Turn left, then right to cross another stile. Cross over the pasture beyond, heading for a metal gate. Continue with hedgerow on your left, soon reaching a large pasture. Now head for the distant oak tree, and when you reach it turn right along a waymarked path. Follow the path to a metalled lane. Turn left, passing a lodge house on the right, and follow the lane to a road junction. Turn right and follow the road, with the brick wall of Glemham House on your right, to reach a T-junction. Now either turn left to head back to All Saints' Church and the end of the walk, or turn right to visit the Crown Inn.

POINTS OF INTEREST:

Great Glemham – There are several interesting buildings in the village. All Saints' Church has a one-handed clock, while the old post office and village store has an old post box and telephone kiosk. Behind the brick wall is Glemham House, home of the Earl and Countess of Cranbrook.

The village lies close to the World War II airfield of Parham, now home to the 390th Bomb Group Memorial Air Museum.

REFRESHMENTS:
The Crown Inn, Great Glemham.

Walk 46   **RENDHAM**   4$\frac{1}{2}$m (7km)

Maps: OS Sheets Landranger 156; Pathfinder 986.

A walk past the site of a famous find.

Start: At 350644, the car park next to the Village Hall, Rendham.

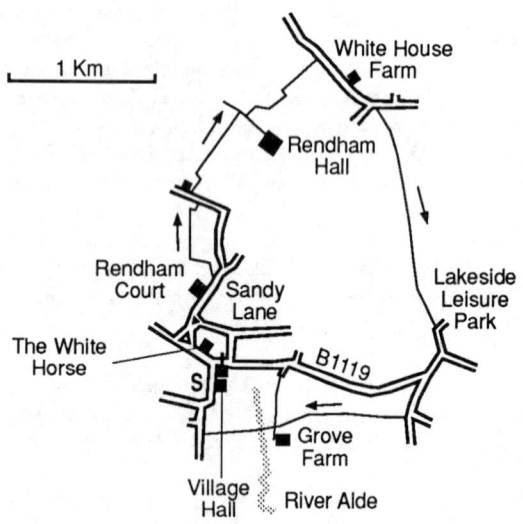

From the car park, turn right to reach the centre of the village and, just in front of the White Horse, turn left to go up Brandeston Road. After a few yards, turn right and go up Chapel Lane. Ignore Sandy Lane, on your right, continuing up the hill past Rendham Court, on your left. Now, just past the driveway to Rendham Court Farm, take the waymarked path on the left, soon bearing right across the field towards the end of a row of poplar trees. Cross a sleeper bridge and follow the left-hand bank of a ditch to reach a concrete bridge. Turn right over the bridge and follow the track beyond into the next field. Turn right and follow the field edge to a road. Turn left along the road and, just before the cottages on the right, turn right along a waymarked path.

Follow the path with the hedgerow on your left, then go through a gap in the hedge and continue in the same direction, but now with the hedgerow on your right. Cross a sleeper bridge into the next field and maintain direction now with the hedge on your left again. At the top of the field, go through the hedge to reach a concrete driveway. Turn right but, just before a pond on your left, turn left to go over a very unique looking stile. Now go past the pond, with it on your right. At the end of the pond you will walk into a field: turn right, and then left to go around the field edge. Now turn right, then left to continue in the same general direction, going along the right-hand edge of a field. Continue in this direction until you reach a metalled lane.

Turn right and follow the lane, passing White House Farm on your left, to reach a road junction. Bear right here to go down a bridleway. Follow the bridleway, with trees on your right, for about 1 mile, passing the Lakeside Leisure Park on your left. Beyond the Park, the bridleway reaches a metalled lane: maintain direction along the road to reach a road junction. Turn right to reach, after 200 yards, the main B1119. Turn left along the road, with care, but after a further 200 yards, where the road turns left, take a bridleway on the right. Follow the bridleway past a pond, on your left, and then downhill to reach a junction of tracks to the right of **Grove Farm.**

Turn right, but after a few yards go left over a stile. Go across the pasture beyond to reach a sleeper bridge crossing the beginnings of the River Alde. Cross and maintain direction, going uphill and passing a plantation on your right. Continue to reach a metalled road. Turn right and follow the road to a junction. Turn right and follow the road back into Rendham village, soon reaching the Village Hall and car park on your right.

POINTS OF INTEREST:

Grove Farm – In 1907 a schoolboy found a bronze head of the Emperor Claudius in the River Alde near the farm. The head is thought to have come from an equestrian statue in Colchester and to have been taken during the sacking of Colchester by Queen Boadicea in 61 AD. The find was sold originally for 5 shillings but much later bought by the British Museum for £15,500. Replicas of the head can be seen in both the Ipswich and Colchester museums.

REFRESHMENTS:
The White Horse, Rendham.

Maps: OS Sheets Landranger 156; Pathfinder 986.

A fine walk through pleasant country.

Start: At 234632, the lay-by in the main road to the south of St Mary's Church, Earl Soham.

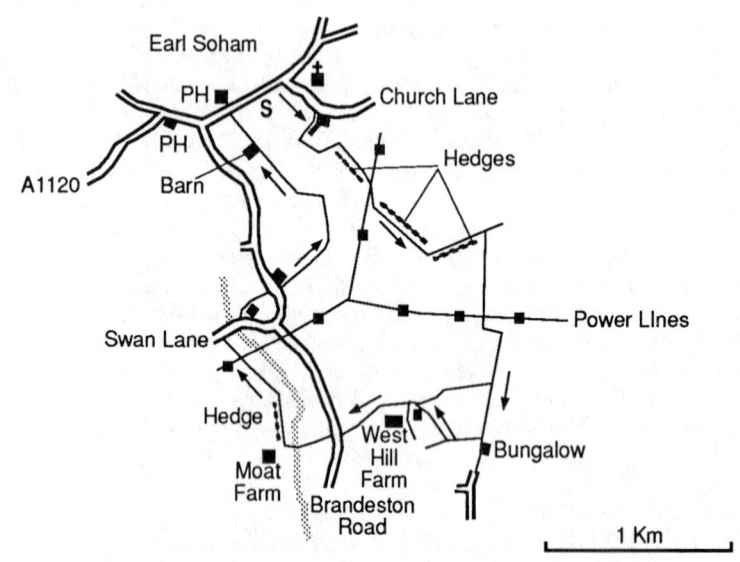

From the lay-by, head towards St Mary's Church. Now, just past the school, on your left, turn right down Church Lane, passing St Mary's Church, now on your left. After some 200 yards, take the waymarked footpath on the right, following it along the left-hand edge of a field. Soon you will reach a gap in the hedge: go through and turn right, now walking with an open field on your left. Continue along the path, soon following it through a hedge again. At the end of the next field you will go back through the hedge again, walking with the hedge on your right once more. Go along the right-hand side of the field to reach yet another gap in the hedge: go through and follow a green track across open fields. Soon after you pass under power lines the track turns left, and then right. Follow the now very distinct track to reach the back garden of the bungalow. Turn right, over a sleeper bridge, and follow the right-hand side of the field beyond. After about 100 yards the path bears right through a gate and goes diagonally across a pasture to the right-hand side of a barn at West Hill Farm. Turn left along the main track and, just past the barn, turn right to go through a gate into a field. Turn left and go through a metal gate into the adjacent field and maintain direction down the field to go through a gap in a hedge on to a track. Turn left and follow the track down to a metalled road (Brandeston Road).

Cross the road and follow the right-hand side of the field opposite, going downhill to reach a wooden bridge over a stream. Cross and follow the right-hand side of the next field up to the corner of Moat Farm. Turn right and follow an indistinct path along the left-hand side of a field, with a hedgerow on your left. The path soon reaches a metalled lane (Swan Lane): turn right, cross a bridge over a stream and then turn left over a stile. Bear right, passing a barn on your right. Follow the right-hand edge of the field to reach a stile and cross to reach Brandeston Road again. Cross the road and follow the path opposite, passing to the right of a bungalow and continuing into a field. Go along the right-hand edge of the field as far as a waymarker. Now turn left across the open field, heading to the left of distant oak trees. Just beyond the trees, bear left and follow a path across a new plantation. Now bear right through another plantation, then follow the path past a barn, on your left, and down to some tennis courts. Continue to reach the main road (the A1120) at **Earl Soham**. Turn right, with care, to return to the lay-by.

POINTS OF INTEREST:

Earl Soham – This charming village is centred on the old Roman Road from Coddenham to Peasenhall. The village takes its name from *Soham* meaning a mere: the last area of marsh was drained in 1970. 'Earl' refers to the village's ownership by the Bigod family of Framlingham, Earls of Norfolk. The village has two public houses, the Victoria brewing its own beer on site.

REFRESHMENTS:
The Victoria, Earl Soham.
The Falcon, Earl Soham.

Walk 48　　　**WESTHALL**　　　$4^{1}/_{2}$m (7km)

Maps: OS Sheets Landranger 156; Pathfinder 946.

A fine walk from a rural Suffolk village.

Start: At 408818, the car park adjacent to the Village Hall, Westhall.

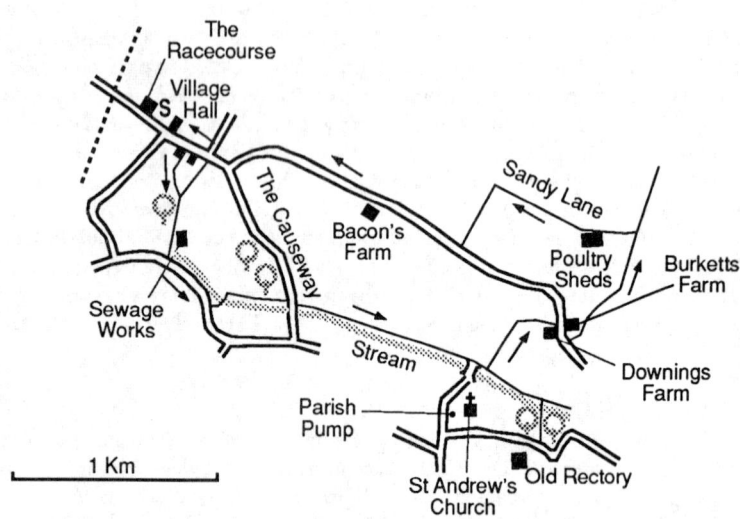

From the car park, turn left and walk past a road junction on the right. After some 150 yards, take a waymarked footpath on the right, going between houses to reach an arable field. Initially follow the right-hand edge of the field, but then, at a corner, bear left and head across the field to reach the end of a line of trees. There, bear right and follow the trees down past a sewage works to reach a metalled lane. Turn left along the lane and, after some 300 yards, turn left to reach a concrete bridge. Cross the bridge and bear right to follow the bank of the stream. Soon you will go through a wood, exiting it to reach a metalled lane (The Causeway).

Cross the lane and continue along the stream bank for another 900 yards or so, going through several fields to reach a concrete bridge on the right. Cross the bridge and follow the lane ahead, passing St Andrew's Church on your left. Continue along the lane, passing the parish pump on your left, to reach a road junction. Turn left and follow the road for about 500 yards, passing the old Rectory on the right, to reach a stile on the left. Cross the stile and head down through the woods. At the bottom of the woods, bear left and cross a ditch into the adjacent field. Turn left and follow the left-hand edge of the field to reach a main track. Turn right up this track to reach a metalled lane.

Turn right along the lane, passing Downings Farm on your right and Burketts Farm on your left. Just beyond the farms, take a waymarked path on the left, following it to the back of Burketts Farm. There, turn right along a track reaching, after some 600 yards, its junction with a green lane (Sandy Lane). Turn left along Sandy Lane, passing poultry sheds on your left, following it to its junction with a metalled lane. Turn right and follow this lane back towards the village of **Westhall**. At the road junction with The Causeway, continue straight on to return to the Village Hall.

POINTS OF INTEREST:
Westhall – The village is situated at the western end of the Wang valley. The Church of St Andrew is surprising large for such a small village, probably indicating a more glorious past. The church is mainly Norman, the north side having been enlarged in the 14th century.

REFRESHMENTS:
The Racecourse, Westhall.
The village stores in Westhall is also a useful source.

Walk 49   LAKENHEATH $4\frac{1}{2}$m (7km)

Maps: OS Sheets Landranger 143; Pathfinder 942.

A walk around Lakenheath, passing the famous airbase.

Start: At 714828, the car park in Wings Road, Lakenheath.

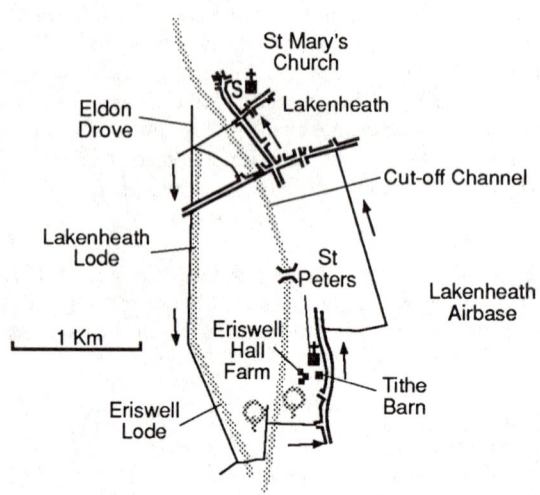

From the car park, turn left to go back into the High Street. Go down the **High Street**, passing St Mary's Church on the left. Just opposite the **Village Green**, turn right to follow a footpath down to the **Cut-off Channel**. Continue along the path to reach a junction of paths. Bear right to cross Eldon Drove and then turn left to go over a stile. Now follow the path going along the bank of Lakenheath Lode (a drain). After some 500 yards you will reach a metalled lane. Cross the lane and continue straight on, passing a farm on the right. After a while the path drops down to the edge of the adjacent field: continue straight on along the path, still following the drain bank (of what is now Eriswell Lode) and eventually reaching a T-junction of paths.

Turn left to go over Eriswell Lode and then, within a few yards, you reach another junction of tracks. Turn left and follow the wide green lane for some 300 yards to where a path goes off to the right. Turn right to go along this path, following it to a bridge over the Cut-off Channel. Cross the bridge and continue straight on to reach the main Eriswell Road.

Turn left and, taking great care along this busy road, follow the main road past Eriswell Hall and the remains of **St Peter's Church**, on the left behind the **barn**. Continue along the road, passing a path on the right. Now take the next path on the right and follow it, with pine trees on your left and a ditch on your right, heading towards the **Lakenheath Airbase**. After some 500 yards the path turns sharp left: turn left with it, following it to reach a metalled lane (Broom Road). Turn left and walk to the High Street. Turn right along the High Street to return to the start of the walk.

POINTS OF INTEREST:

High Street – Some of the buildings in the High Street date back to the 17th century. Part of St Mary's Church dates from the 15th century.

Village Green – This is the remains of the village's South Green, where the village pond was once situated. It was filled in after World War II.

Cut-off Channel – The channel was built to control flooding of the River Lark. It joins the River Lark at Barton Mills and allows flood water to flow into the River Ouse at Denver near Kings Lynn.

St Peter's Church and Barn – Situated in Little Eriswell the church was converted into a dovecote in the 18th century. The Tithe Barn beside the church was built in 1754.

Lakenheath Airbase – This was originally Lakenheath Warren on Lord Iveagh's Estate. During World War I it was used as a training area for the newly developed tanks. During the early part of World War II it was used as a decoy airfield for RAF Feltwell. Since 1948 it has been home to the USAF and now deploys the 48th Tactical Fighter Wing. It can be a very noisy place!

REFRESHMENTS:

There are several possibilities in Lakenheath.

Walk 50   SAXMUNDHAM   4¹/₂m (7km)

Maps: OS Sheets Landranger 156; Pathfinder 986.

An interesting walk from Saxmundham to Kelsale.

Start: At 387631, Somerfield Stores, Saxmundham.

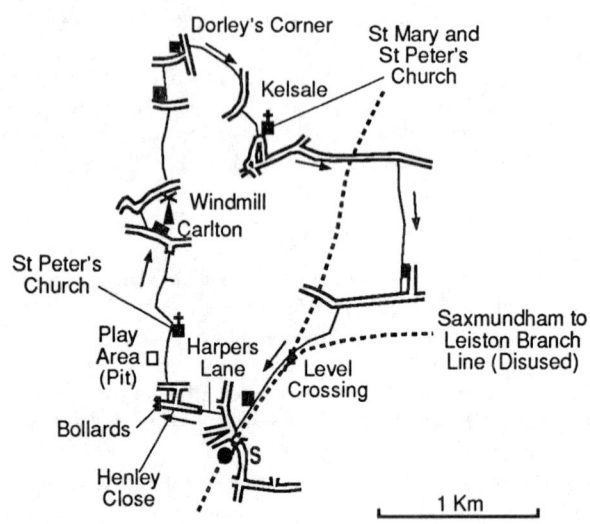

From the entrance to Somerfield Stores, go along the driveway to reach the High
Street opposite the Queen's Head. Turn right along the High Street, passing the Market
Place on your left and going under the railway bridge. Just past the second turning on
the left, you will reach Harpers Lane. Turn left along this lane, which soon becomes
a metalled path and leads into Henley Close. Go along this, passing a turning on the
right (Felsham Rise). Now, just before reaching some bollards across the road, turn
right along a footpath. The path soon crosses a bridge and reaches a metalled road:
cross and follow the path opposite up to a sports ground.

     Bear to the right of a pit (play area) and head towards St Peter's Church, Carlton.
From the front of the church, take a path which soon crosses a stream, on your right,
and then becomes a trackway. Follow the track to a metalled lane. Turn left to reach,
after a few yards, a village green. Take a path on the right and follow it to the left of

96

a row of cottages. The path soon reaches a metalled lane on a corner: turn right and follow the lane past an old windmill. Just past the windmill, turn left and follow a footpath along the right-hand side of an open field. Soon the path crosses a ditch and then continues along the left-hand edge of another field. Turn right at the end of this field and, after a few yards, turn left to go through some scrub to reach a metalled lane.

Cross the lane and follow the path opposite, going past a small pond on the left and continuing to reach another metalled lane. Turn right and follow the lane to reach the Saxmundham road at Dorley's Corner. At this road junction, take the path opposite, following the left-hand bank of a stream to reach a lane. Turn right and then, after 100 yards, turn left to follow the path up to Kelsale Church. Bear to the right of the church and follow the path to reach some steps that lead to a lane. Turn left and follow the lane, passing the old school house on the left, to reach a T-junction. Turn left and follow the lane (Bridge Street) past the Methodist Church, on the right. Soon the road bears to the right (Lowes Hill) and crosses the Ipswich to Lowestoft railway line: after a further 200 yards, turn right along a waymarked path, walking with hedgerow on your right.

Continue along the path, passing a barn on your left to reach a metalled road. Turn right and, after some 500 yards, turn left along a waymarked, cross-field path to reach the distant railway bank. Turn right and follow the railway (the disused **Leiston Branch Line**) to reach a level crossing at its junction with the main line. Cross the main line, with care, and turn left to follow the track to the main road, passing a farm house on the way. The path here may be a little overgrown. At the main road, turn left and go under a railway bridge to return to the High Street and the end of the walk.

POINTS OF INTEREST:

Leiston Branch Line – This branch line was opened in 1859 and was only intended to go as far as Leiston where Richard Garrett, an East Suffolk Railway director, had his world famous engineering works. However, with funding from Sir Samuel Peto the line was extended, in 1860, to Aldeburgh in order to open up the then fishing village to tourism. This part of the line was never really successful, due mainly to the position of the station at Aldeburgh, and the whole line closed to passenger traffic in 1966. The Leiston branch remained open for goods traffic during the building of Sizewell nuclear power station.

REFRESHMENTS:

There are numerous opportunities in Saxmundham.

Walk 51   **KERSEY** $4^1/_2$m (7km)

Maps: OS Sheets Landranger 155; Pathfinder 1029 and 1030.

A walk through pastures and around Kersey.

Start: At 001442, the main street in Kersey.

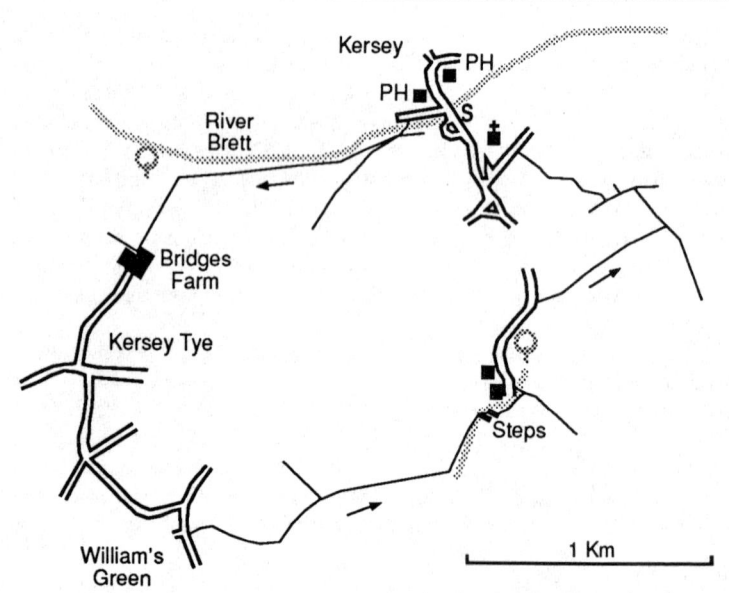

Street parking is available in Kersey, but please park considerately.

From the main street, go down the lane between the Bell and the stream (the River Brett). At its end, go over a stile on the left and head down to a bridge over the stream. On the far side of the bridge, turn right and follow the bank of the stream, soon passing through a metal gate. At the end of the next field, bear left to go through another metal gate. Now continue along the right-hand side of a pasture to reach a barn on the right. Turn left to follow a track for some 500 yards, soon passing through Bridges Farm and continuing to reach a metalled lane. Follow the lane to reach a road junction in Kersey Tye.

Now maintain direction, soon crossing another road junction, and continuing to a T-junction at William's Green. Turn right and then, just past a house on the left, turn left to follow a path along the left-hand side of an open field. Soon the path bears left into a wood, goes through the wood and leaves it with a hedgerow on the right. Continue in the same general direction to reach a large open field. Here, head downhill along a cross-field path, heading towards a waymarker – which is hard to see at first – in the distance. At the bottom of the field you will reach a track: turn left and walk to a bridge over the stream on your right. Go over the bridge and then, after a few yards, climb up the bank on the far side by means of some crudely cut steps.

At the top of the bank, turn left and follow the edge of the field to reach a junction of paths just past a house on the left. Turn left and cross a bridge over the stream, then turn right to continue along a metalled driveway. Just after the end of the woods on your right, turn right to follow a path along the side of a stream. After some 600 yards you will reach a junction of paths: turn left and follow a cross-field path to reach a metalled lane. Turn left and, after passing a driveway on your right, turn right along a path. The path goes, initially, along the left-hand side of an open field, and then crosses the field to reach a metalled lane. Turn left and, just past the church on the right, turn right along a narrow lane, soon passing Kersey primary school, on your left, and **St Mary's Church**, on your right. Continue along the path from the church to return to the start of the walk in **Kersey**.

POINTS OF INTEREST:

St Mary's Church – This 14th/15th-century church has been restored many times but still has a wealth of interest. Look, especially, for the decorated panelled roof of the East chapel and the hammerbeamed roof of the nave.

Kersey – The village is often said to be one of the most beautiful in Suffolk, or even England. Kersey prospered greatly in the 15th century with the growth of the wool trade in the area and is said to have given its name to 'Kersey Cloth'.

REFRESHMENTS:
The Bell, Kersey.
The White Hart, Kersey.

HAWKEDON   4¹/₂m (7km)

Maps: OS Sheets Landranger 155; Pathfinder 1005 and 1006.
A fine walk across fields and around the village of Hawkedon.
Start: At 798530, the Village Hall, Hawkedon.

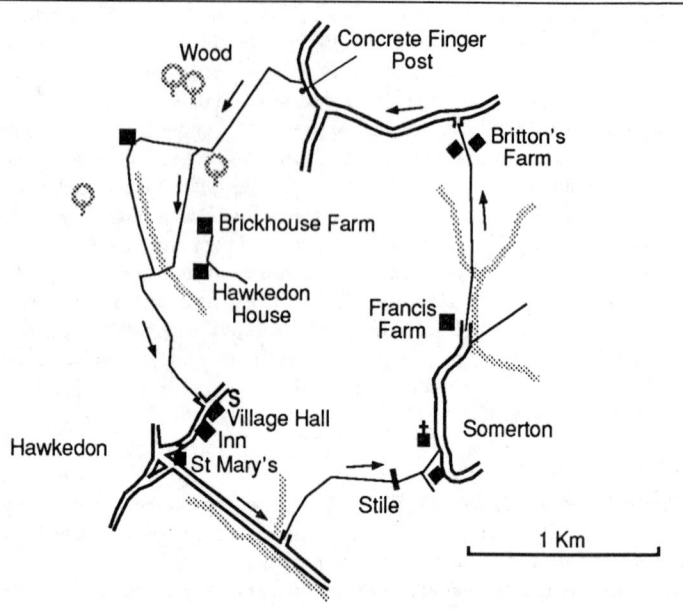

From the front of the Village Hall, turn left to go down to the village green and
St Mary's Church. Cross the green in front of the church and turn left along a metalled
lane. After about 700 yards you will reach a bridge over a stream and a trackway on
the left. Turn left along the trackway to reach a gate. There, bear right along the side
of a field, heading towards Somerton Church in the distance. Soon you will reach a
stile: go over into an arable field and cross the field heading for a house in the distance,
to the right of the church. At the far side of the field, turn left and head towards the
church. The path soon reaches a metalled lane in Somerton: turn left, passing
St Margaret's Church on the left. The church will probably be locked, but the key is
available.

Go past Church Farm and continue along the lane, soon going downhill and around to the left to pass Francis Farm on the left. Just beyond the farm buildings, keep straight on, initially with a stream on your right. Cross a bridge and continue, with the stream now on your left. Cross an arable field, and continue, soon reaching Britton's Farm. Go through the middle of the farmyard and continue to reach a metalled lane. Turn left and follow the lane down to a road junction.

Turn right and, after a few yards, turn left at a concrete waymarker to follow the right-hand side of an open field. Turn left in the corner of the field and walk to the end of the hedgerow. The path now goes across the field heading for the left-hand side of a copse. Keep straight on to cross a ditch and then turn left, and then right, into an adjacent field. The 'path' in this field is indistinct: follow the left-hand side of a hedge, going uphill to reach the corner of the field. Turn left and follow the field edge downhill to reach a stream, with Hawkedon House on your left. Cross a bridge slightly hidden amongst the undergrowth to reach a trackway. Turn left and follow the trackway back into **Hawkedon**. At the end of the trackway, turn right to return to the Village Hall and the end of the walk.

POINTS OF INTEREST:
Hawkedon – Typical of a once thriving agricultural village that has now declined due to changes in agricultural practice and improved road communication. Hawkedon has two manor houses, Thurston Hall and Hawkedon Hall, which still conjure up an atmosphere of medieval life.

REFRESHMENTS:
The Queen's Head, Hawkedon.

Walk 53   **BRANDESTON** $4^3/_4$m ($7^1/_2$km)

Maps: OS Sheets Landranger 156; Pathfinder 986.

A walk through Cretingham golf course and past Brandeston Hall.

Start: At 249606, the Queen's Head, Brandeston.

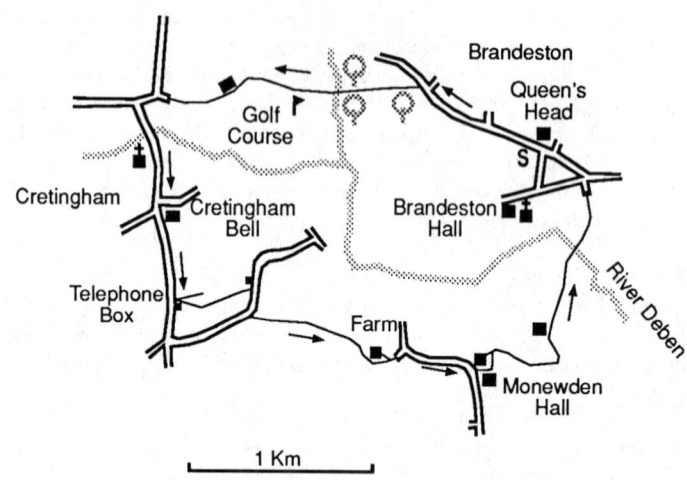

From outside the Queen's Head, walk into Brandeston along The Street, passing the Old Laundry House on the left. Just past the second turning on the right, take the footpath on the left, going over a stile and then walking to the right of some woods. At the end of the wood, cross a stile and continue down the side of a field to reach another wood. Continue straight on, soon crossing a wooden bridge into the Cretingham Golf Course.

Cross the first fairway reached and maintain direction, soon passing the 4th green. Now walk up to the side of the 1st tee, and then follow a track, passing the golf clubhouse on your right. Continue along the track to reach a metalled road. Turn left, with Manor Barn Farm on your left, soon reaching a road junction. Turn left and follow a lane which soon crosses a bridge over the River Deben. Soon after crossing the bridge you will pass St Peter's Church on your right. Continue to the crossroads with the Cretingham Bell on the left, and there keep straight on, going uphill until you reach a telephone box on the left.

Turn left and follow the left-hand side of an arable field, soon crossing a wooden bridge over a ditch. Continue straight on to reach the corner of the field. Now keep straight on along a cross-field path, heading for the right-hand side of a distant house. Just beyond the house you will reach a metalled lane: turn right, but after a few yards, where the road turns sharp right, turn left to follow another cross-field path, this one heading for a distant corner of the field. Now walk along the right-hand side of a hedgerow, following the edge of the field.

Soon the path turns right: continue along it to reach the right-hand side of a farm building. Here the path joins a track that is followed to a metalled lane. Turn right and follow the lane for some 500 yards to reach Monewden Hall. Now, just after the lane turns sharp right, take the bridleway on the left, following it between the Hall, on your right, and a barn, on your left. Go straight across a grassy area to reach a small gate. Go through, turn left, and then right to join a main track. Follow this track downhill and then left to pass a remote cottage, on your left. Continue along the track, which soon crosses a bridge over the River Deben. Now follow the track to reach a road opposite a road junction. Turn left and follow the road towards All Saints' Church and **Brandeston Hall**. Just before the Hall, turn right and follow the lane back to the Queen's Head and the start of the walk.

POINTS OF INTEREST:
Brandeston Hall – The Hall was built in 1543 for the Revett family who continued to occupy it until 1809. The Hall is now an independent boarding school.

REFRESHMENTS:
The Queen's Head, Brandeston.
The Cretingham Bell, Cretingham.

Walk 54   ORFORD CASTLE AND THE RIVER ORE   5m (8km)

Maps: OS Sheets Landranger 156 and 169; Pathfinder 1009.
A circular walk around Orford.
Start: At 425496, the harbour car park, Orford.

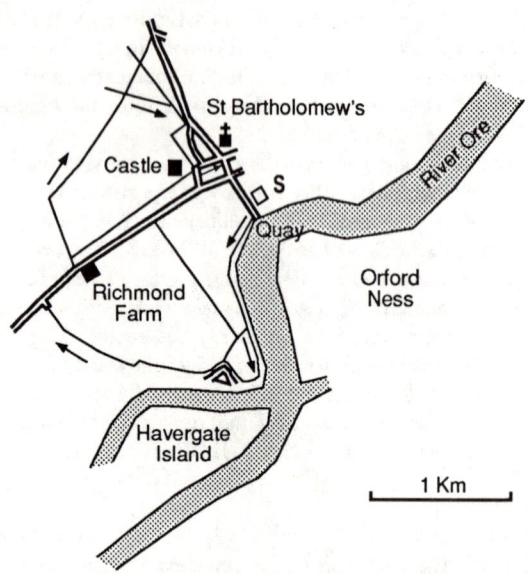

From the car park exit, turn left down to the quay, passing the Old Warehouse Tea Rooms on your left. At the quay, turn right along the sea wall, passing mud flats and **Orford Ness** on your left. Continue along the sea wall, passing the northern end of the **Havergate Island** bird sanctuary, then, where the sea wall turns sharp left, take the path on your right signposted for Richmond Farm and Orford. The path leads to a track: follow this to reach a road. Turn right along the road, but, after about 200 yards, opposite Richmond Farm, turn left along a track. Follow the track past a barn on the right, then bear right just before a conifer plantation. Continue along the track to reach some cottages on your left. Turn right at a waymarker and follow a path towards **Orford Castle**.

The path leads to a track behind the fire station: turn right and walk past the school. Turn right again into the recreation ground and cross it aiming for the castle. When you reach a track in front of the castle, turn left down to the castle entrance. Turn left at a metalled road, following it back into Orford, passing the Orford Museum and the Crown and Castle Hotel. Continue down the hill, passing **St Bartholomew's Church** before returning to the car park.

POINTS OF INTEREST:
Orford Ness – The curiously elongated peninsula of Orford Ness is not accessible to the general public. However, it is no longer used by the Atomic Weapons Research Establishment and a bird reserve is now being created so the situation may change in the near future. The aerials seen on the peninsula are used by the World Service of the BBC for transmissions to Eastern Europe.
Havergate Island – The island is a bird reserve managed by the RSPB and is famous for being the place where the avocet first returned to breed in Britain in 1947. It is not open to the public, but special access may be obtained by contacting the warden.
Orford Castle – This is one of the most important medieval castles in England. It was built by King Henry I between 1165 and 1173. King Edward III gave it to the Earl of Suffolk in 1337 and it remained in private hands until it was given to the Orford Town Trust in 1930. In 1962 it was taken over by the Ministry of Works and is now in the care of English Heritage.
St Bartholomew's Church – Orford Church was rebuilt in the 14th century on the ruins of an earlier church built by King Henry II.

REFRESHMENTS:
There are no refreshments en route, but there are possibilities in Orford.

Walk 55   THORPENESS AND SIZEWELL   5m (8km)

Maps: OS Sheets Landranger 156; Pathfinder 1009.

A walk from an Edwardian village to a modern day power station.
Start: At 472595, the car park beside the Gallery Tea Rooms,
Thorpeness.

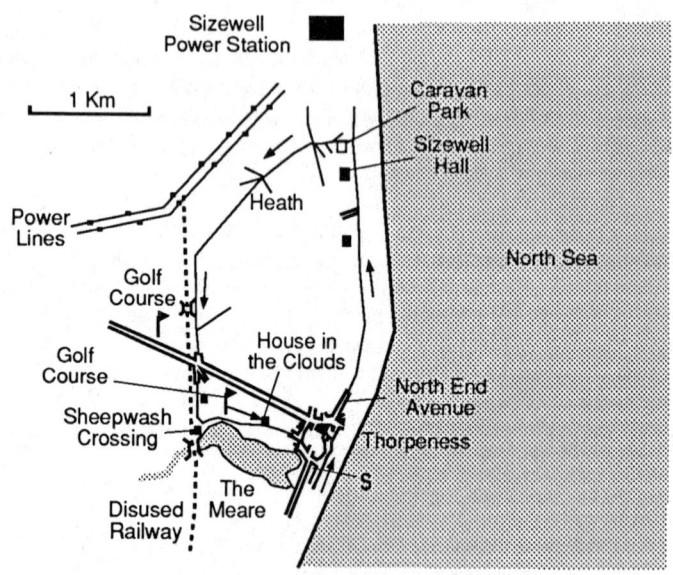

Leave the car park by the back exit, towards the sea, and turn left along a metalled
lane. Go past Drake House and then turn right into the Coastguards (road) which soon
becomes a track, passing a church on the left. The track then joins a small lane: turn
right and head towards North End Avenue. At the end of the avenue, a path continues
along the cliff top. Beyond a small clearing, the path goes down the cliff and proceeds
along the back of the beach. Walk along the beach and eventually back along the cliff
top, passing a walled garden to reach a junction of paths. Ignore the path on the left
and continue along the path waymarked as the Suffolk Coastal Path.

    Soon you will reach the walled garden and ornate bridge of Sizewell Hall.
Continue along the path and then turn left at the end of a caravan site. Follow the path
to a lane beside the main entrance gates to Sizewell Hall Christian Conference Centre.

Cross the lane and follow the path going into a heath next to a telephone pole. (Ignore the main path on the left). Continue along the path, initially heading towards two pylons in the distance, to reach a green lane. Turn left along the lane to reach a junction of paths at the start of a heath. Now ignore the main sandy track on your right, continuing straight on along a lesser path to the left of a line of hawthorn bushes, the remains of a hedgerow. The path may be slightly overgrown, but improves as it continues between two wire fences on the edge of the heath. After some 700 yards the path meets a crossing path by a stile.

Do not cross the stile: instead, continue for another 200 yards to reach a junction with a wider path. Turn left down the path, walking beside the course of a disused railway. After 500 yards, cross a track that goes under the railway by a disused railway bridge. Keep straight on here, following the path to a road. Cross the road and take the right-hand track running along the edge of the golf course. Pass to the right-hand side of a barn and continue, later passing to the left-hand side of a house and joining another path at a disused level crossing (Sheepwash Crossing). Turn left and follow the path with The Meare on your right and the golf course on your left. The path soon passes to the left of the golf club house: head between the **House in the Clouds**, on your left, and a **windmill**, on your right. Follow the path to a road and turn right to head back to the car park and the end of the walk.

POINTS OF INTEREST:
The House in the Clouds/Windmill – The original windmill was located at Aldringham some 2 miles away. In 1922 it was decided that the village water pump and tank were unsightly and arrangements were made for the Aldringham windmill to be moved to its present site. The mill was converted into a water pump when the House in the Clouds was erected as a storage tank, with accommodation below. The pump was in use until World War II, and the House in the Clouds remained in use until 1963 when mains water was provided to the village. The mill is now a Visitors Centre while the House in the Clouds is rentable holiday accommodation.

REFRESHMENTS:
The Dolphin, Thorpeness.
The Gallery Tea Rooms, Thorpeness.

Walk 56 TRIMLEY MARSH AND THE RIVER ORWELL   5m (8km)

Maps: OS Sheets Landranger 169; Pathfinder 1054.

A walk beside Trimley Marsh Bird Reserve.

Start: At 277357, the car park beside Searson's Farm, Cordy's Lane, Trimley St Mary.

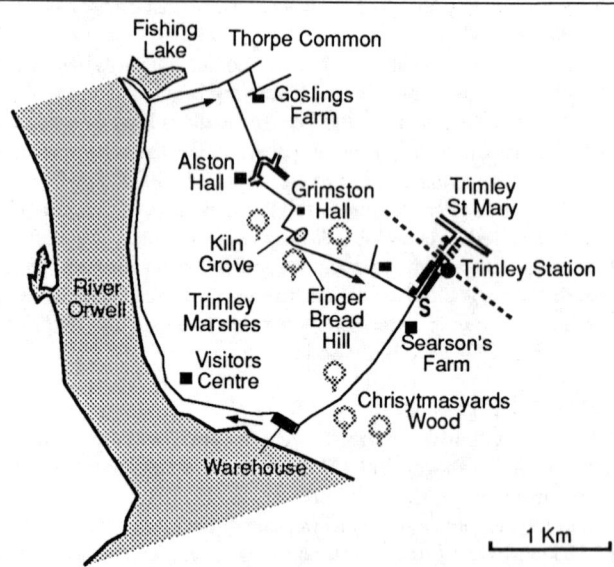

From the car park, to the right of Searson's Farm, follow the bridleway south towards the River Orwell. The track soon passes through Christmasyards Wood (a narrow woodland strip) and then goes down to the edge of the Felixstowe Docks expansion. For a view across the docks continue along the track, following the sign to Flagbury Cliff. The route continues by turning right and following the track signposted Suffolk Wildlife Trust Nature Reserve. This track passes to the right of a new wooded bank hiding large warehouses. Beyond, the track soon turns left towards the river and then right again along the river. At this point an alternative path is available, going along the top of the sea wall. This alternative offers views across the water to Shotley Gate and the ex-naval training school (HMS Ganges) on your right and Harwich and Parkeston quay on your left.

Continue along either the track or the sea wall path to reach the edge of **Trimley Marshes Bird Reserve**. This Reserve was constructed in 1986, financed by the Felixstowe Dock Company, to create bird feeding grounds as a replacement for the estuary mud flats destroyed by recent docks expansion.

Soon after you pass the Reserve's Visitors Centre the sea wall path becomes difficult to follow and it is advisable to continue along the lower track. The track follows the river bank at first, then heads inland slightly, going uphill and then descending to the edge of a fishing lake. Just before the lake turn right up a track heading towards Thorpe Common and Goslings Farm. At the top of a slope, turn right along a track between Scots pines. The track soon reaches a metalled lane: turn right and head towards Alston Hall. Just beyond a cottage on the right, turn left and follow the track to **Grimston Hall**. Turn right just in front of the Hall and follow the track heading towards the river. After 200 yards, bear left along a path through Kiln Grove and follow it down to a pond. Now follow the path up Finger Bread Hill and along a newly planted avenue of trees to reach the keeper's lodge. Now ignore the track on the left, keeping straight on past the lodge, which is also on your left, and continuing along a gravel track. The track soon reaches Cordy's Lane: turn right to return to the car park.

POINTS OF INTEREST:

Trimley Marsh Bird Reserve – The Reserve has several hides open to the public and can be accessed from the main track. The Visitors Centre is open on Mondays, Wednesdays, Saturdays and Sundays from 10.00am to 4.00pm. It is managed by volunteers from the Suffolk Wildlife Trust.

Grimston Hall – This private farmhouse was the birthplace of Thomas Cavendish (1555-1592), the second commander to circumnavigate the world.

REFRESHMENTS:

There are no refreshments actually on the walk but coffee, lunches and drinks can be obtained in Trimley St Mary.

Walk 57   **WALBERSWICK AND TINKERS MARSH**   5m (8km)
Maps: OS Sheets Landranger 156; Pathfinder 966.
A windswept walk across Tinkers Marsh.
Start: At 499749, the Ferry Lane car park, Walberswick.

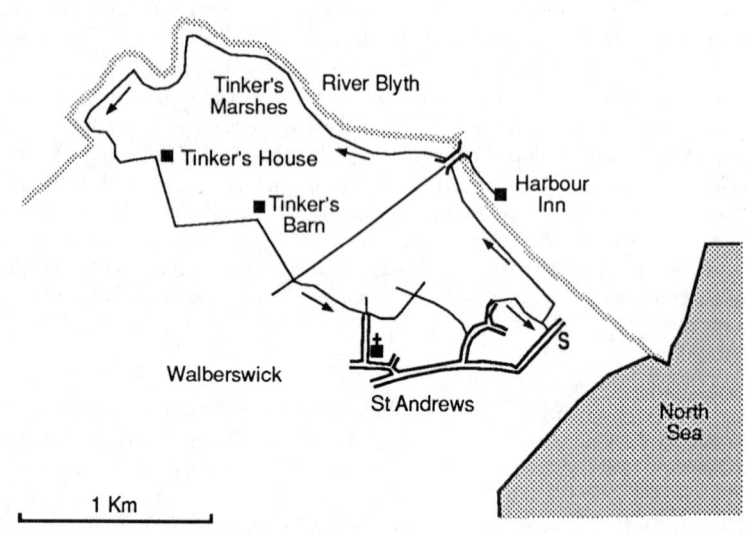

This walk, although very scenic, is exposed to easterly winds. Warm clothing is therefore advisable.

From the car park, follow a waymarked, paved path towards the river and continue along the river wall, heading westwards towards Blythburgh. After about 900 yards you will reach the course of the old Halesworth to Southwold light railway, where it crossed the river: continue straight on into Tinkers Marsh Nature Reserve. The path follows the river wall and care must be taken with your footing in the long grass. After about 1½ miles the path heads south-westwards, still following the river, and in the distance you can see Blythburgh Church. Soon the path leaves the river and heads inland towards an isolated house (Tinkers House).

Cross a stile and head towards the house. The path turns right and passes to the right of the house: from the front of the house continue along a track going inland, heading in a southerly direction with a hedgerow on your left. After 300 yards the path turns sharp left and heads towards another isolated house (Tinkers Barn), with Southwold lighthouse in the distance. Follow the path over a stile and head towards St Andrew's Church, Walberswick. The path soon cuts across an embankment of the old railway: turn left, go through a field gate and then turn right to continue in the same direction, with the church now slightly on the right. Continue past a football field, on your left, and the backs of houses, on your right. The track on your right that goes between the houses leads to St Andrew's Church and **Walberswick**.

Continue along the path, which soon reaches some houses and a metalled road. Turn left along the road and then slightly right to go along a green track. This track is soon crossed by a path: turn right along the path, following it to another metalled road. Turn left along the road, but, after some 100 yards, turn left again along a green waymarked track, following it down to a field gate and stile. Cross the stile and turn right to follow the field edge past a reed bed, on your right, to reach another stile, ignoring the small stiles leading to some of the back gardens. Cross the stile and head up the bank to reach a paved path. Turn right to return to the car park.

POINTS OF INTEREST:

Walberswick – This was once a thriving fishing port but suffered, as did many other east coast ports, from silting of the harbour. The fortunes of Walberswick can be seen in the history of St Andrews Church, especially in the building of the large nave in 1493 and its destruction in 1695.

REFRESHMENTS:

There are several possibilities in Walberswick.

Walk 58   DEDHAM AND FLATFORD MILL   5m (8km)

Maps: OS Sheets Landranger 155 and 168; Pathfinder 1053.

A walk along the River Stour via Flatford Mill.

Start: At 058333, the car park in front of Dedham Vale Rare Breeds Centre.

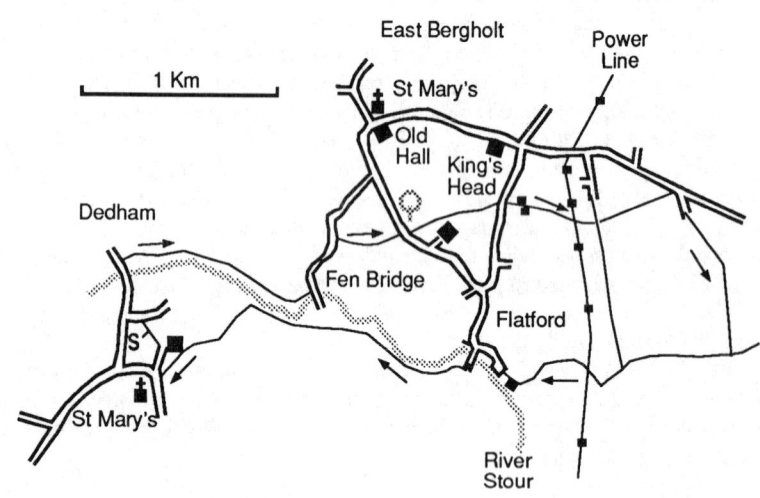

From the car park, leave by the entrance to the Rare Breeds Centre, crossing a bridge and then turning left. Follow the path to reach a track. Turn left and cross a stream by a ford. At the main road (the B1029) turn right, with care. Cross two bridges and then take the footpath on the right, following it along the River Stour, with the river on your right. The path follows the bank of the river to a bridge (Fen Bridge). Do not cross the bridge: instead, follow the track to your left, soon reaching another bridge. Here the track bears left, but you go straight ahead, over a stile. Bear right to follow the path beyond the stile uphill to reach a stile and track. Cross the track, maintaining direction to walk into a plantation, soon passing a water treatment works on your right. At the bottom of a hill, cross a bridge and follow the path beyond up to a metalled lane.

From here you can turn left and go up the hill to reach **East Bergholt** and the King's Head.

To continue the walk, cross the lane and follow a waymarked path to Clapper Farm House. Cross a field to your right to reach another track, turning left between farm buildings. Now continue along the right-hand side of a pasture to reach a stile, ignoring a waymarked path on the right. Cross the stile and follow the right-hand side of an arable field, passing an electricity pylon and continuing to reach a metalled lane.

Cross to waymarked path opposite and follow it along the right-hand side of a pasture. Go across another field and then along a path between two houses to reach a road. Turn right and, within a few paces, turn right again to follow a wide track past houses on your right. Follow the track to reach an open meadow. Now turn right and follow the hedge on the right, going over several stiles and past the end of a green lane (to Ovis Farm). Continue straight on: soon the path turns right and then goes left at an electricity pylon to reach a stile. Beyond, the path enters the National Trust property of **Flatford Mill**.

Turn right along a grassy track to reach a group of cottages (Willy Lott's Cottage) and continue past Flatford Mill. Both these sites are part of a Fields Studies Centre. Go past Valley Farm, on the right, and tea-rooms, on the left. Now turn left to go over a bridge and take the path on the right to go along the left bank of the River Stour. Continue along the path, passing Fen Bridge on your right, to reach a double stile and bridge over a drainage ditch. Continue along the path beyond to reach Dedham Hall Farm and the main road. Turn sharp right down a track to Dedham Hall and then take a path on the left, going past a small lake to return to the entrance to the Rare Breed Farm Centre and the car park.

POINTS OF INTEREST:
Flatford Mill – Dedham, East Bergholt and Flatford Mill are all places associated with the painter John Constable. Flatford Mill is owned by the National Trust and houses exhibitions on and by the artist.

REFRESHMENTS:
The King's Head, East Bergholt.
The Marlborough Head Inn, Dedham.
The Sun Hotel, Dedham.
Teas and coffee are also available at Flatford Mill.

Walk 59 STUTTON AND THE RIVER STOUR 5m (8km)

Maps: OS Sheets Landranger 169; Pathfinder 1053.

A short dry walk through woods along the River Stour.

Start: At 143348, the car park outside the Stutton Community Hall.

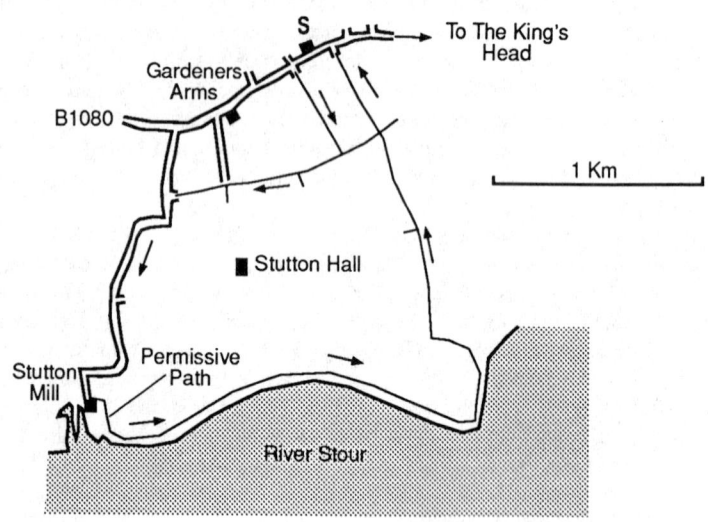

Leave the car park and turn right along the main road (the B1080). Soon, turn left down a footpath which soon becomes a farm track (Manor Lane). At the end of the track, turn right and follow the track through Manor Farm. Continue past trees, on your left, soon reaching the main drive way of Stutton Hall. At this point you can turn right and head back to the main road for refreshments at the Gardeners Arms.

To continue the walk, carry straight on along the track to reach a T-junction. Turn left and follow the well-defined track down to Stutton Mill and the river. At Stutton Mill the public right of way goes past the front of the Mill, but there is also a permissive path at the back of the buildings.

Either route reaches the river: turn left and follow the river's edge, with Stutton Hall on your left and Parkeston quay just visible at the far end of the river. Soon you will come to the edge of a wood and a stile: cross the stile into the wood, continuing along the river's edge. Cross a wooden bridge just by a clearing and continue along the path, keeping straight on where the main track veers left, inland. At the far side of the wood, cross a stile into an arable field and continue along the river's edge to reach Stutton Ness. To the right, across the river, is Essex.

At Stutton Ness the path turns left and becomes a grassy track: continue along it. Soon, the track turns sharp left and heads inland to reach Crepping Hall Farm. At a gate across the track, keep straight on, passing the farm building and house on your right. Continue along the main track, soon reaching another track on your left. Keep straight on, passing between an avenue of black poplars and holly to reach the main road again. Turn left and follow the road back to **Stutton** and the Community Hall.

POINTS OF INTEREST:
Stutton – At the time of Doomsday, the village had six manors, evidence of which can still be seen today. Alton Hall, one of the manors, is now more associated with Alton Reservoir which provides drinking water to the surrounding area as well as sports and leisure activities.

REFRESHMENTS:
The Kings Head, Stutton, at the start/finish of the walk.
The Gardeners Arms, Stutton.

Walk 60   BELSTEAD   5m (8km)

Maps: OS Sheets Landranger 169; Pathfinder 1030.

A circular walk around Belstead village.

Start: At 131410, the car park at Belstead village hall.

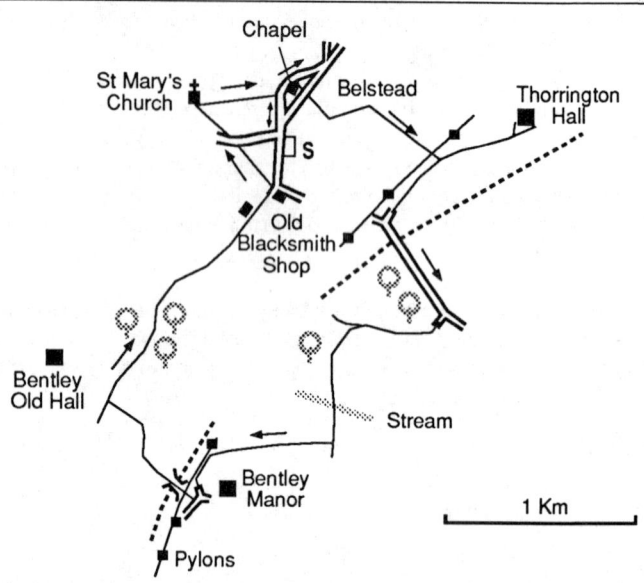

From the village hall, turn right and walk up to the old village school. Where the road bears right at a junction, keep straight on along the minor road to pass to the left of the school. Follow the road around a right-hand bend and then take the footpath on the right, just past the old Wesleyan Methodist Church. The path passes between houses and soon reaches the Ipswich Road. Cross and follow the path opposite into an open pasture. Soon the path leads down to open heathland and woods: continue along it through the open woodland to reach a large open field. Now turn left along a permissive path around the edge of the field, with woodland on your left.

At the top of a slope the path continues straight on across an open field, heading towards the radio masts at Wherstead: stay with it to reach a major track going down to Thorrington Hall. Turn right and head uphill – away from the Hall – following the line of the electricity pylons. Follow the track to a metalled lane and turn left along it. Cross the bridge over the main London to Ipswich railway line and continue along the lane, passing Wherstead Woods on your right.

Just at the end of the woods, turn right along a bridleway, following it around the outside of the woods and downhill to reach the right-hand corner of a field. Keep straight on into the woods, but immediately bear left along the bridleway and go downhill to reach a small stream. Continue along the bridleway, uphill, until you come out to a field on your right. Now turn right along the right-hand side of the field, with the hedgerow on your right, following a track on to a metalled lane going to Bentley Manor. Turn right along the lane and then right again to follow a path towards the railway bridge. Cross the bridge and go straight on, through a young plantation and along a track heading towards Old Hall in the distance. On reaching a junction of tracks, turn right and walk through woodland, keeping straight on at all times until you head along Bentley Lane and join the corner of a metalled road at the old blacksmith's shop.

At the corner, take the path to your left, crossing a field diagonally and heading towards **St Mary's Church**. Cross a metalled lane and continue towards the church. At the church, turn right and follow the left-hand edge of the field, passing between houses to reach a metalled (Chapel Lane) in Belstead. Turn right to reverse the outward route to the car park at the village hall.

POINTS OF INTEREST:
St Mary's Church – Unfortunately the church is kept locked, but a note on the door explains where the keys can be obtained.

REFRESHMENTS:
None en route, the nearest being in Washbrook, a mile or two westwards.

Walk 61   CHELMONDISTON AND PIN MILL   5m (8km)

Maps: OS Sheets Landranger 169; Pathfinder 1054.

A walk along the River Orwell.

Start: At 204374, St Andrew's Church, Chelmondiston.

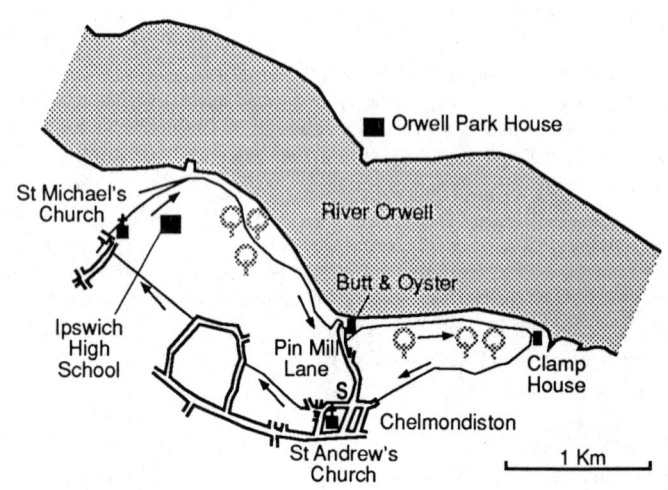

Car parking is limited, but space should be available in the main street and Church Road. Please park thoughtfully.

Starting from the entrance to St Andrew's Church (in Church Road), follow the lane opposite and, where it bears to the right, continue along a bridleway into open pasture. On the right there are fine views across the river to Orwell Park, the home of the 19th-century engineer and land owner George Tomline who built the railway from Ipswich to Felixstowe.

Go across the pasture and down to a metalled lane. Turn right and follow the lane past Pages Common. Keep straight on at a track junction, following the lane past houses on the right. Now, where the lane turns to the left, keep straight on along a bridleway signposted to Freston. Slightly to the right you can see St Michael's Church, Woolverstone and the tower of Ipswich High School for Girls.

Follow the left-hand edge of the field, soon crossing a pasture and the tree-lined approach to Ipswich High School. After crossing the driveway, bear right to head towards St Michael's Church. Pass to the left of the church, passing some magnificent beech and hornbeam trees, and bearing right to pick up a waymarked path heading into the woods on your right. Follow the path downhill to arrive at the entrance to Woolverstone Marina and the Royal Harwich Yacht Club.

Follow the track down to the river and turn right to follow a riverside path, eventually bearing right into woodland. Follow the path through the woods and along the river to reach a junction of paths. Turn left to follow the river towards Pin Mill. **Pin Mill** is an ideal spot for a break at the Butt and Oyster.

The route continues up the road, passing a car park on the right, and then goes up concrete steps on the left. Follow the path between houses to reach the Pin Mill Cliff Plantation, given to the National Trust by Mrs Maud Rouse in memory of her husband. Continue along the path through the plantation, ignoring all paths on your right to eventually reach the end of the plantation at Clamp House. Now take the track on the right and follow it uphill, heading back to Chelmondiston. At the farm, keep straight on, going downhill to reach Pin Mill Lane. Cross the lane and go along Hollow Lane to return to St Andrew's Church.

POINTS OF INTEREST:

Pin Mill – The character of Pin Mill has changed little over the years. It is well-known all around the world as a haven for sailors, and is equally well known for its public house, the Butt and Oyster. Arthur Ransome, the author of *Swallows and Amazons*, spent a lot of time at Pin Mill and based the story *We Didn't Mean to Go to Sea* on the area.

REFRESHMENTS:
The Butt and Oyster, Pin Mill.
There are also possibilities in Chelmondiston.

Walk 62   IXWORTH AND THE TWO MILLS   5m (8km)

Maps: OS Sheets Landranger 155; Pathfinder 963.

A circular walk passing two ancient mills.

Start: At 932703, the Village Hall car park, Ixworth.

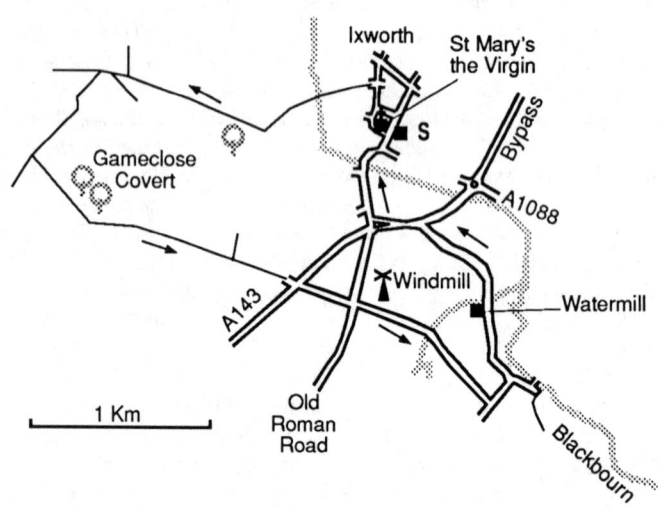

From the car park, go back to the High Street and turn left, then right to reach **St Mary the Virgin's Church**. Go to the left of the church, passing the cemetery, and continue to Commister Road. Turn left and follow the road around to the right. Just by Abbey Close, take the bridleway opposite, going along the tree-lined way to reach Hempyards Bridge over the River Blackbourn. Notice here, on the left, a lovely native black poplar tree.

Cross the bridge and head towards a small wood. Turn right and follow a track along the edge of a field for about 1,000 yards and, at the end of a small plantation, turn left along a bridleway heading for the edge of a small copse. Go along the right-hand side of the copse and continue along the track. The track soon turns sharp left and then passes to the right-hand side of Gameclose Covert: continue along it, passing through an orchard and then along Heath Lane to join the main A143.

Cross, with care, and go along Cutter's Lane to reach the **windmill** on the junction with the old Roman Road to Ixworth. Cross the Roman Road and continue along Thieves Lane. Go over Fulmer Bridge and continue to the junction with Fen Road. Turn left and then, after passing some houses, turn left again, heading towards **Pakenham Watermill**. Follow the lane to its junction with the A413. Turn left and then right, crossing the main road with care and following the old Roman Road back into Ixworth to return to the start.

POINTS OF INTEREST:

St Mary's the Virgin Church, Ixworth – A church was recorded on this site in the Doomsday Book (1086). The present building dates from the 14th century and has some fine flintwork patterns on the 16th-century Tower.

Pakenham Windmill – This well-known landmark was built in 1816 and restored to full working order in the 1950s. It is open to the public by appointment.

Pakenham Watermill – This 18th-century watermill was restored by the Suffolk Preservation Trust. It is open to the public from 2.00pm – 5.30pm on Wednesdays, Saturdays, Sundays and Bank Holiday Mondays from Good Friday to the end of September.

REFRESHMENTS:

There are several possibilities in Ixworth.

Walk 63　　REDGRAVE AND LOPHAM FENS　　5m (8km)

Maps: OS Sheets Landranger 144; Pathfinder 964.

A very pleasant walk through the village of Redgrave and the Lopham Fens.

Start: At 046779, the village green, Redgrave.

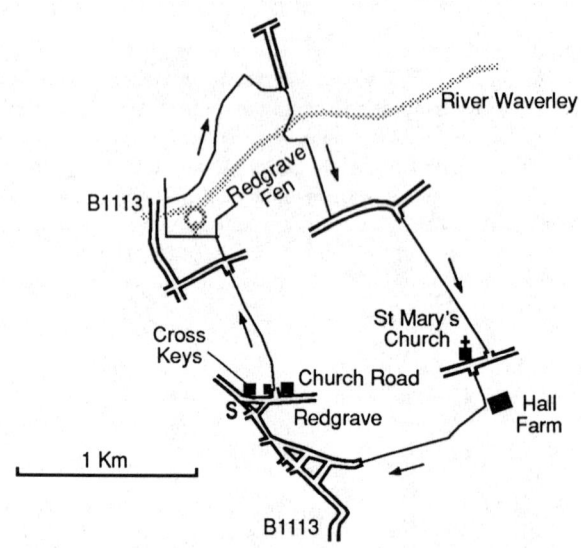

Starting the walk from outside the Cross Keys, turn left and left again to go down Church Road. After some 100 yards, take the waymarked track on the left, going between some houses and continuing past an open field, and then woodland, on your right. Go past a cottage and then down to a metalled lane. Cross the lane and follow the path into **Redgrave and Lopham Fens**.

At the start of the fen there is a Nature Reserve information board showing a map of the fens. Our route will take us along part on the main fen walk which is waymarked with a white arrow.

Just beyond the information board, turn left along a well-trodden track along the left-hand edge of the wood. Just before you come to a road (the B1113) the track turns right: follow the track and turn right again through a metal gate. (This area is the source of the River Waveney). Continue along the track, following the white arrows, to soon reach a bridge. Cross the bridge and continue to follow the white arrows to reach the main car park area for the Reserve.

Take the path in the far right-hand corner of the car park (heading south next to the information board) and follow the white arrows down to the river. Turn right and then, soon, left to go over a bridge. Bear left for some 500 yards to reach another information board. Turn right to exit the woods, going along a track that reaches a road. Turn left along the road, passing Pine Street Farm on the left. Fresh asparagus can be bought at the farm in season.

Where, after a double bend, the road turns left, keep straight along a track heading to the left of **St Mary's Church.** The track soon reaches a metalled road: turn right towards the church. Opposite the church, turn left and follow the track up to Hall Farm turning right just before the building. Now follow the track to soon reach a metalled lane. Continue along the lane, passing many fine houses, until you reach the main road (the B1113). Turn right to return to the Redgrave Village Green.

POINTS OF INTEREST:

Redgrave & Lopham Fens – These valley fens are managed as a Nature Reserve by the Suffolk Wildlife Trust and are the largest remaining tracts of valley fen left in England. The 123.5 hectare site is internationally important for its variety of habitats, including sedgebeds, reedbeds, wet heaths, open water and woodland. The fen is one of the few remaining sites where the fen raft spider can still be found. Sadly the spider is threatened by the lowering of the water level due to over extraction from a nearby borehole.

St Mary the Virgin Church, Redgrave – The church was originally the chapel of a Benedictine Nunnery and now contains one of the finest collections of hatchments in the country.

REFRESHMENTS:
The Cross Keys, Redgrave.

Maps: OS Sheets Landranger 156; Pathfinder 966.

A fine walk along the River Blyth and a disused railway.

Start: At 452755, the lay-by north of the Holy Trinity Church, Blythburgh.

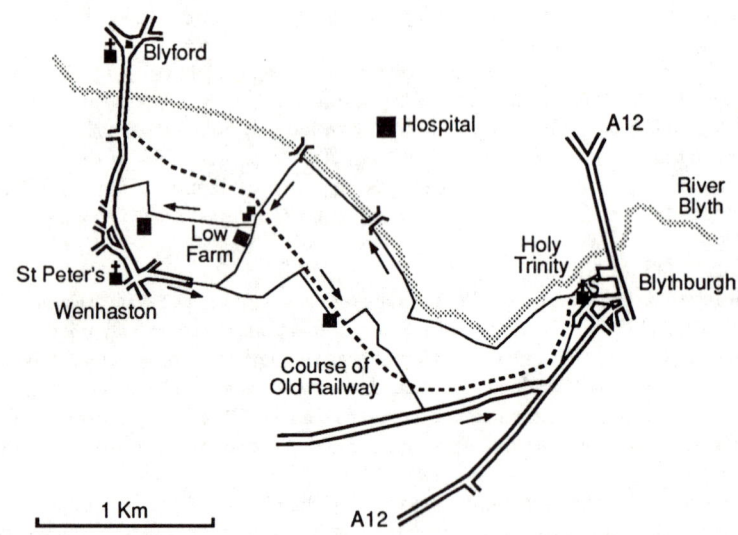

From the car park, follow the track past a metal barrier and along the course of the old Halesworth to Southwold Railway. Just before reaching the back of Holy Trinity Church, bear right to follow a path along the southern bank of the River Blyth. Continue along the bank to reach a bridge over the river. From here you can see Wenhaston on your left and Blyford Church straight ahead.

Continue along the south bank of the river until you reach the next bridge and turn left there to follow the right-hand edge of a field to a small wooden bridge. Cross the bridge and follow the left-hand edge of the field beyond to reach a second bridge. Cross and walk to the left-hand corner of the next field, where there is a stile on the left. Cross the stile and bear right to reach a stile beside a metal gate. Cross the stile and follow the track beyond, passing Marsh Cottage on your right.

Just after a small garage, also on the right, take a path through a gap in the conifer hedge and bear right around the edge of the field beyond to reach its far corner. Go through a gap in the hedge and follow a cross-field path towards a distant oak tree. At the oak tree, turn right and head towards a shed on the far side of the field. At the shed, turn left and follow the path along the left-hand side of a bungalow to reach a metalled road. Turn left along the road, following it into Wenhaston.

Just opposite St Peter's Church, turn left along a lane, following it for some 900 yards, passing a cemetery on the right. Where the road turns sharp right, carry straight on, crossing a stile. Turn right to follow the course of the railway, soon reaching a wooden gate across the track. Turn left in front of the gate and cross a stile. Follow the track beyond around to the right and cross a bridge to reach another stile. Cross, turn left and walk towards the next stile. From this stile, follow the left-hand edge of the field to reach a further stile. Do not cross this stile: instead, bear right across the field to reach another stile, cross and bear left towards a gap in the distant hedge. Go through on to a metalled road. Turn left along the road to reach the busy A12.

Turn left, with care, and, after a few yards, turn left again to go along a path to **Holy Trinity Church**. From the front gate of the church, take the path on the right-hand side, following it down to the river. There, turn right and follow the track back to the car park.

POINTS OF INTEREST:
Holy Trinity Church – Known locally as the 'Cathedral of the Marshes', Holy Trinity is a magnificent, 15th-century priory church and amply characterises Blythburgh's prosperous past. It has fine stonework and wood carvings and is well worth a visit.

REFRESHMENTS:
The White Hart Inn, Blythburgh.
The Compasses Inn, Wenhaston.
The Star Inn, Wenhaston.
There is also a Post Office and General Stores in Wenhaston.

Maps: OS Sheets Landranger 155; Pathfinder 1006.

An interesting walk around Hartest.

Start: At 832525, the car park behind the W.I. Centre, Hartest.

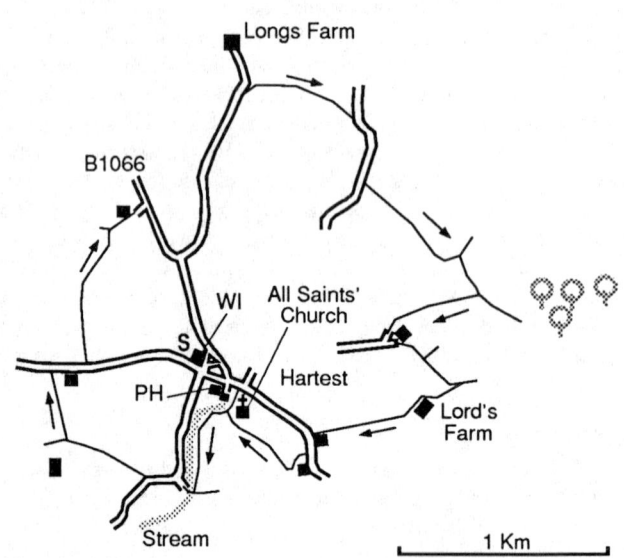

From car park, turn left and go down to the main road (the B1066). Cross, with care, and follow the lane opposite, with the war memorial on your left. Just beyond the Crown, follow the track between the public house and the church, soon crossing a small bridge over a stream. Continue to a fork in the path: take the right-hand branch, following the bank of the stream with an arable field on your left. Stay with the stream, ignoring a bridge on your right and continuing to reach a trackway. Turn right, but, within a few yards, turn right again to follow a short lane to a road.

    Turn left and follow the road for some 150 yards to reach a right-hand bend. There, turn right along a waymarked path, with a hedgerow on your right and an open field on your left. Continue along the right-hand edge of the field to reach its end and bear right there to follow the left-hand edge of the next field, now with a hedgerow on your left. At the end of this field, take a path on the right, soon reaching a metalled lane. Turn right and, after passing a house on the right, turn left to walk downhill along a track. Continue along this track to where it divides, then take the right-hand fork, passing a bungalow on your left. Follow the track to reach a metalled road (the B1066).

Turn right along the road and, after some 350 yards, where the road bears left, then right, turn left along a lane. The lane soon leads to open fields: continue to a point just before Longs Farm, at a bend in the lane, and there turn right along a waymarked track. Follow the track, with a hedgerow on your right, and then, at the top of a hill, continue with hedgerow on your left. Soon you will reach a metalled lane: turn right and follow the lane for 400 yards to reach a waymarked path on the left. Follow this path, going along the edge of arable fields to reach a corner of a gravel track. Keep straight on along the track and, just before a wood on the left, take a path on the right, walking with a hedgerow on your right.

Follow the path down to reach the right-hand side of a cottage and, just beyond, a metalled lane. Turn left along the lane which soon becomes a gravel track. Follow the track to a junction of tracks and turn right there, heading towards Lord's Farm. Just before the farm buildings, take a path on the right bypassing the farm. Follow the path down the left-hand side of open fields to reach a metalled road. Turn left and then, just before Pippin Cottage, turn right along a waymarked path. At the bottom of a slope the path bears right and follows the right-hand side of a open field: just before the far corner of the field take a path on your right to reach the bridge crossed earlier in the walk. Now reverse the outward route to return to the start in **Hartest**.

POINTS OF INTEREST:

Hartest – An interesting feature of this delightful village is Hartest Stone, a glacial stone standing on one corner of the green. It was placed there to celebrate the signing of the Treaty of Utrecht at the end of the War of Spanish Succession in 1713.

REFRESHMENTS:
The Crown, Hartest.

Walk 66　　　**SANTON DOWNHAM**　　　5m (8km)

Maps: OS Sheets Landranger 144; Pathfinder 943.

A lovely walk through heathland and forest.

Start: At 816878, the car park next to village shop in Santon Downham.

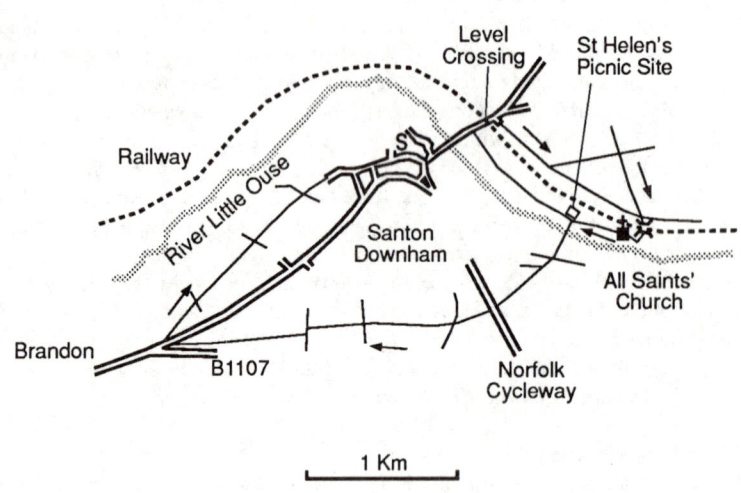

From the car park, turn left to follow the metalled lane down to the bridge over the River Little Ouse. The river here marks the boundary between Norfolk and Suffolk. Go over the bridge and along the lane to reach a level crossing. Just beyond the crossing, turn right along a forest trackway, walking with the railway on your right-hand side. After some 500 yards, take the track off to the left, going past a post marked "21" on the corner. Follow the track as it goes slightly uphill to reach (after about another 500 yards) a junction of tracks. Turn right and follow this now grassy track downhill to reach the railway again.

Turn left, but within a few metres turn right to follow a path under the railway. On the other side of the railway, bear right along a track, passing to the right of All Saints' Church, Santon. The church is unlocked and is worth a visit. Continuing along the path you will soon reach St Helen's picnic site, with a new toilet block on the right. This is a very popular picnic site in the summer and is accessible by way of the road through Santon Downham. It could, of course, be used as an alternative start for this circular route.

Turn left and follow a path to a wooden bridge over the river. You are now back in Suffolk having strayed into Norfolk. Continue to reach a T-junction of tracks. Turn right and, after a few yards, take the next main track on the left to climb uphill to a tarmaced road (the Norfolk Cycleway). Cross the road and continue straight on, following a path back into the woods to reach another track. Turn left and then, within a few paces, turn right to continue in the same general direction. Go across another track, continuing to reach a T-junction. Turn left and then, after about 100 yards, turn right and follow a path out to a metalled road, reaching it at its junction with the B1107.

Cross the road and turn left. Now, after a few yards, turn right and follow a path into the woods. Stay with this path for about 1 mile, crossing several wide tracks to reach some new houses on the edge of **Santon Downham**. Now maintain direction along the metalled lane, keeping to the left at all times and soon returning to the village shop and the end of a very enjoyable walk.

POINTS OF INTEREST:

Santon Downham – The village is in an area of East Anglia called Breckland. This area is heathland – i.e. it has a sandy, well-drained, nutrient poor soil – that traditionally supported sheep and rabbits. In the 1920s the Forestry Commission purchased many old estates and started planting conifers. These trees are indigenous to the area and thrive on the light soils. However, due to the loss of grazing/browsing animals many of the indigenous heathland plants and associated wildlife are threatened with extinction.

REFRESHMENTS:

The only opportunity is the village shop in Santon Downham.

Maps: OS Sheets Landranger 144; Pathfinder 963.
A walk along the "Grundle".
Start: At 964735, the Village Hall car park, Stanton.

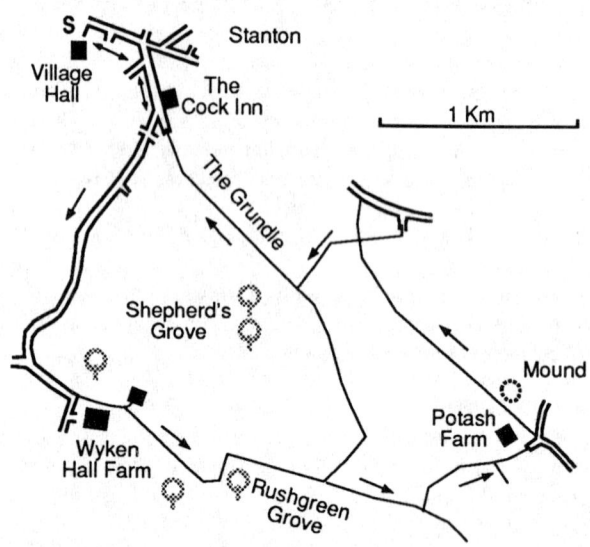

From the village hall car park, where toilets are available, go back to the main road, turn right and follow it, with care, into Stanton. Bear right to pass **All Saints' Church**, on your right, and follow the lane (The Street), soon passing the Cock Inn on your left. Continue on along Wyken Road, soon passing Wyken House on the left.

Soon you will reach a road junction: continue straight on, heading towards Wyken Hall Farm. Where the road turns sharp right, continue straight on, passing the farm buildings on your right. Just beyond a large barn, bear left, and then right, to walk along the right-hand side of a large arable field. Continue around the edge of the field until you pass the edge of Rushgreen Grove, on your right. Now, in the corner of the field, turn right and follow the edge of the wood, soon reaching a trackway with ditches to the left and right. The track soon comes out into open fields: continue along it to reach a major track on your left. Turn left and follow this track around to the front of Potash Farm.

Just past the farm the track reaches a metalled lane: turn left and, within a few yards, left again along a path. Follow the path, soon passing a high mound on the right, to reach its junction with a trackway. Turn left. Follow the track for about 300 yards to where it turns sharp right, with a path on the left. There, turn right, now with a hedgerow on your right, but within a few yards follow a waymarked path into the "**Grundle**". Continue along this path for some 900 yards to reach a track, continuing along the track to reach a metalled lane (The Street). Turn right and reverse the outward journey back to the Village Hall.

POINTS OF INTEREST:

All Saints' Church – Stanton has two medieval churches, All Saints' with its beautiful ogee tomb-arch and St John the Baptist with its fine 14th-century windows. All Saints', passed on the walk is the only one now in use. The Church of St John the Baptist is roofless and has only one token service each year.

The Grundle – This is a local name for a gully or gorge cut into the underlying chalk. There are several grundles in Suffolk and such gorges are also known as "Gulls".

REFRESHMENTS:
The Cock Inn, Stanton.

Walks 68 & 69   BUNGAY   5m (8km)
                                  or 10m (16km)

Maps: OS Sheets Landranger 134 and 156; Pathfinder 945.
A walk around the meadows of Bungay to Mettingham Castle.
Start: At 336896, the Priory Lane car park, Bungay.

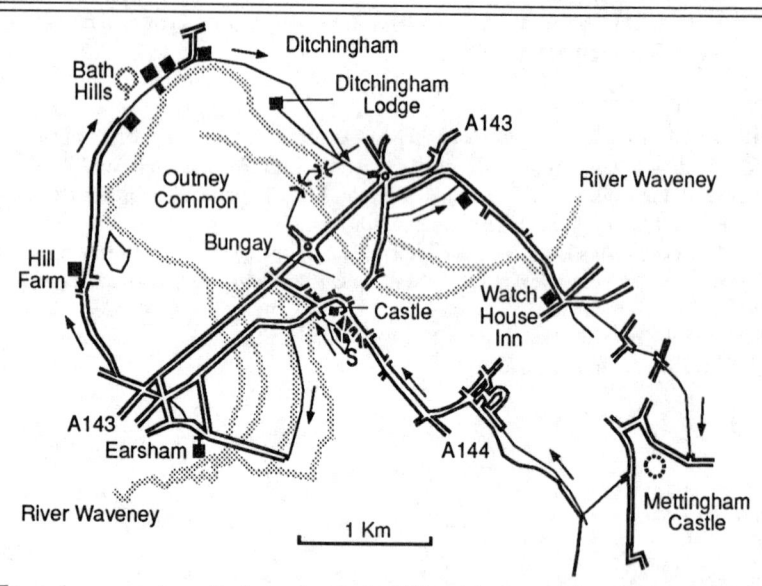

From the car park, walk down to Castle Hills and take the footpath on the right, following it to reach Earsham Road. Turn left and follow the road over the River Waveney. Just before the next bridge, turn left and follow a path down the left-hand side of a channel to reach All Saints' Church, Earsham. Just beyond the church, take a path on the right, following it between houses to reach The Street. Cross The Street, go along Station Road and cross the bypass, with great care, into the road opposite. After a few yards, turn right into Bath Hills Road and follow it, passing gravel pits on your right, to reach Valley Farm. Maintain direction, but then bear left just before some farm buildings to go uphill along a grassy track. Soon you will reach a metalled lane with houses to the left and right. Continue uphill and, where the road bears sharp left, go straight on, following a pleasant path along the top of the hill. Just beyond the driveway of Ditchingham Lodge you will reach a junction of paths.

The shorter route turns right here, following a path over two narrow bridges. Now follow a track over a marsh, go over another bridge and follow a trackway towards a roundabout on the Bungay bypass. Just before the roundabout, turn right and follow a path, with the bypass on your left. Cross a footbridge over the bypass and continue along Outney Road heading back into Bungay to regain the start of the walk.

The longer route turns left and follows the path to reach the roundabout at the eastern end of the bypass. Bear right, cross the bypass, with care, and follow a lane, with Simpson's Maltings on your left. Go over a bridge and, just after a T-junction on the left, turn left to follow a path across a pasture. Maintain the same general direction across several fields to reach a metalled lane (Wainford Road). Turn right and follow the lane to a junction of roads, with the Watch House on the right. Turn left to go along the main road, with care, and, after some 200 yards, turn right to follow a path uphill. Follow the path to a metalled lane. Bear right along the lane, but where it turns right, keep straight on along a track with hedgerows to both left and right. Soon the track reaches a lane: bear right, then left to continue along an old sunken trackway. Follow the track to a metalled lane and turn right to go past Mettingham Castle, on the left. After a further few yards, bear left at a road junction and then go left again at a second junction. After 400 yards, and just before a house on the right, turn right along a sunken lane. At the end of this lane turn right and follow the right-hand edge of a ditch for some 800 yards to reach the end of a road on a housing development. Follow the road to a T-junction. Turn left and, after a few yards, turn left again to go between houses and across a yard to reach a main road. Turn left and follow the road to its junction with the main A144. Turn right and follow the road back into **Bungay** and the start of the walk.

POINTS OF INTEREST:

Bungay – There are many places of interest in Bungay, particularly the remains of the, mainly 13th-century, castle, the 17th-century Buttercross and the many Georgian houses. The Otter Trust at Earsham, south-west of Bungay, is also worth a visit. An animal-lovers paradise, the Trust provides a refuge for otters and other animals in a tranquil setting beside the River Waveney.

REFRESHMENTS:

The Watch House, on the longer walk.
There are also numerous possibilities in Bungay and Earsham.

Walk 70   **BRANDON**   5¹/₄m (8¹/₂km)

Maps: OS Sheets Landranger 144; Pathfinder 942.

A walk along the River Waveney.

Start: At 785868, the Co-op car park, Brandon.

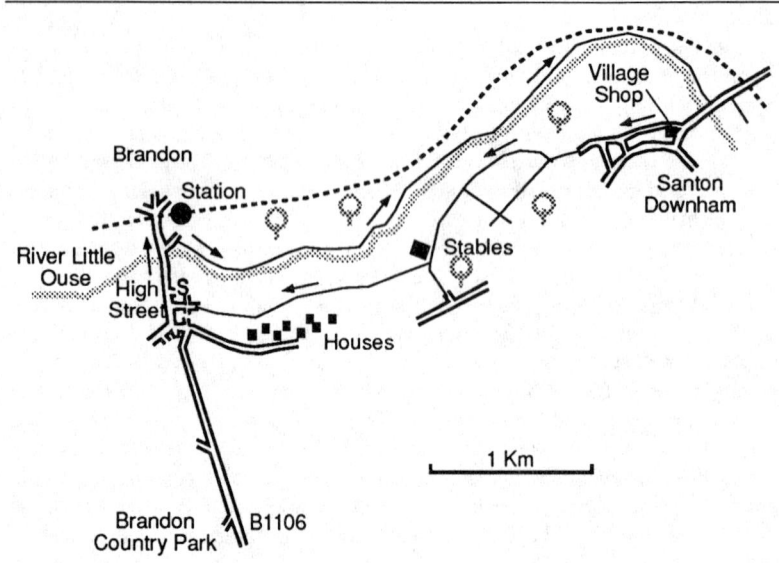

From the car park, turn right along the High Street and follow it down to the bridge over the River Waveney. Cross the bridge and turn right down Riverside Way. After a few yards, turn right again to follow a path down to the river. Now follow the riverside path for almost 3 miles, all the way to the next bridge at the village of Santon Downham. The riverside path might be a little overgrown in places, but it never leaves the riverbank. Some of the ground covered is difficult however, and care should be taken.

    When you reach the bridge, go up the steps, turn right to cross the bridge and follow the lane into Santon Downham. Just before the Post Office and Stores, turn right and follow a metalled lane. Where the lane bears left, keep straight on, soon passing the 'Old Billiard Room' on the left. At the next junction, keep straight on, following a track into the forest. Once in the forest, take the first trackway reached on the right and follow it to reach a major track on the left at the Suffolk County Council Campsite.

Keep straight on, soon reaching a riding centre on the right. Turn right at the next junction of tracks, just beyond the riding centre. Follow the track for about $1\frac{1}{4}$ miles, going past the backs of houses before reaching **Brandon**. At the end of the trackway (which is now called Gas House Drove), turn right, then go left to return to the starting car park.

POINTS OF INTEREST:

Brandon – Once famous for its flint knappers, the village has grown immensely since the end of World War II. It is now a both a light industrial town and a popular retirement area.

Brandon Park, situated on the Elvedon road, was built for Edward Bliss in 1826. The estate in now owned by Suffolk County Council and run as a Country Park. The house has been restored and is now a hotel.

REFRESHMENTS:

There are possibilities in both Santon Downham and Brandon.

Walk 71   FRAMLINGHAM CASTLE   5$\frac{1}{2}$m (9km)

Maps: OS Sheets Landranger 156, Pathfinder 986.

A circular walk from Framlingham Castle.

Start: At 285635, the car park beside Framlingham Castle.

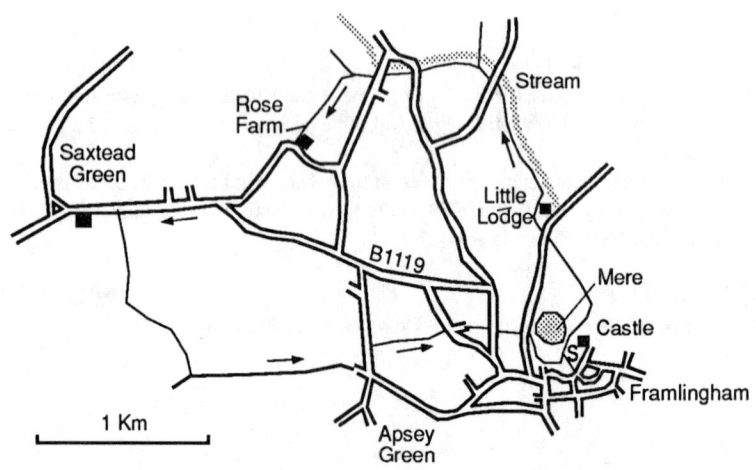

On leaving the car park, turn right past the Castle Inn and right again along a waymarked track going downhill to the mere. At the bottom of the hill, go through a gate and turn right, following the path around the mere. Soon, the path heads towards Framlingham College sports ground: cross a stile into the college sports ground and maintain direction across the field beyond, heading for a waymarker at the side of a road. Cross the road and follow a waymarked path around the back of 'Little Lodge' passing a paddock on your right. Cross the stile at the corner of the paddock and go downhill towards some farm buildings. Turn left at edge of the buildings and follow the edge of a field, keeping a stream on your right. Eventually you will reach a road: continue along the waymarked path opposite, again following the stream on your right.

Soon you will cross another road. Crossing into the opposite field, turn right to go around the field edge, keeping a band of trees on your right. The path, which might be ploughed, leads to a track which is followed past Rose Farm and on to a small lane. Turn right and follow this lane to a junction with the Saxted Green to Framlingham road (the B1119). Turn right and follow the edge of the road, with care, for about 200 yards, then take a waymarked path on your left at the end of the village green. Cross a stile into a pasture and then go over another stile continuing along the edge of the field beyond to reach a bridge. Now maintain direction to reach the bridleway in the distance. Follow the bridleway, still heading in the same direction.

The bridleway soon turns sharp left and follows the edge of a field: at the bottom of a slope, turn left at the junction with another bridleway and follow the new track for about 1,000 yards to reach the road at Apsley Green. Turn left along the road but, after about 200 yards, turn right along a waymarked path. Follow the path across a field to reach another road and continue down the turning opposite. At the bottom of the road take a footpath between houses. This path leads to another road with a view of **Framlingham Castle** opposite. Cross the road and follow the path opposite down to a gate at the edge of the mere. Turn right and follow the path around the mere, passing a car park and eventually reaching the track used earlier in the walk. Now reverse the first few yards of the walk to return to the start.

POINTS OF INTEREST:

Framlingham Castle – Framlingham was once an important medieval town and has lots of interest to offer the walker, especially the Church of St Michael and the Castle. The castle, now in the care of English Heritage, remains virtually as it was when it was built in the 12th century. The continuous curtain wall links 13 towers and offers magnificent views of the town and mere. At various times the castle has been used as a prison and a school. The castle, which also houses a small museum of local history, is open to the public during standard opening times.

REFRESHMENTS:

There are numerous possibilities in Framlingham.

Walk 72   **ALDEBURGH**   5$\frac{1}{2}$m (9km)

Maps: OS Sheets Landranger 156; Pathfinder 1009.

A circular walk going along the coast to North Warren, back along a disused railway and then down to the river.

Start: At 466571, near Moot Hall.

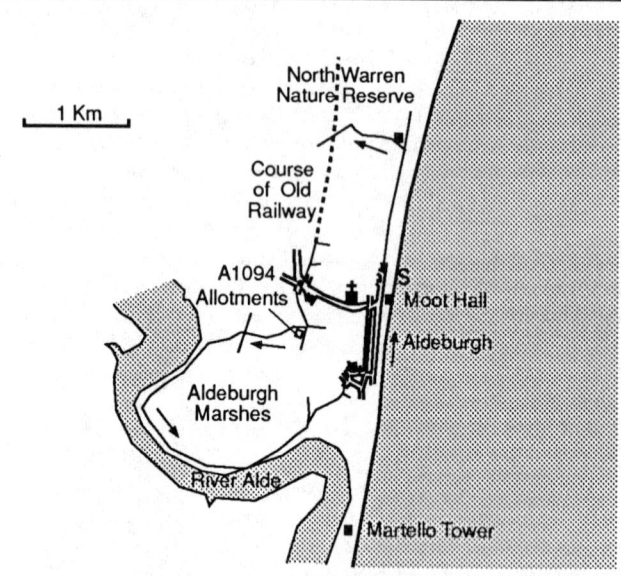

Please park carefully on the street near Moot Hall.

From Moot Hall take the tarmaced path along the sea front, heading north towards Thorpeness and Sizewell. After about 1,000 yards the path ends by a seat and a cottage on the left: cross the road and take the waymarked path into the **North Warren Nature Reserve**. Although this is a marsh/wet meadow the path is raised and dry. Follow the raised path across the marsh to reach the embankment of the old Saxmundham to Aldeburgh railway branch line.

Turn left to follow the old railway track back towards Aldeburgh. After about 1,000 yards you will reach the edge of a caravan site, on your left, and housing, on your right: maintain direction along a narrower path which soon reaches a metalled road (Church Farm Road). Turn left and follow the road to a roundabout. Cross Church Farm Road and the main road (the A1094) with care, bear right and then turn left to follow the path down to the fire station.

Go past the fire station and over the recreation ground, heading towards a brick wall on your left. Follow the path beside the brick wall and then turn right to go into allotments. Pass through the middle of the allotments, go over a bridge and then cross a second bridge into a meadow. Maintain direction across three fields to reach a waymarker and a concrete bridge. Cross the bridge and bear slightly left to head towards a gate and stile. Now continue to reach the river wall. Turn left and follow the wall for about $1^1/_2$ miles to reach steps going down from the wall on your left. At this point you can take a diversion to see the **Martello Tower** off to your right.

To continue the walk, go down the steps and follow the track over a bridge towards the town. Where the track divides, take the right branch, following the track to reach Park Road. Turn right and, at the end of Park Road, turn left to head back into town along the High Street, **Aldeburgh**. At any time you can now turn right to reach the promenade and then go left to return to Moot Hall.

POINTS OF INTEREST:
North Warren Nature Reserve – This is one of the oldest nature reserves managed by the RSPB. The area is mainly a wet grazing meadow and reed bed with the contrasting dry acid grassland and heath and so provides a very diverse habitat for plants and animals.
Martello Tower – The tower that stands to the south of the town was one of 75 built in 1810-12 as part of the country's defences against a Napoleonic invasion. The towers were a copy of the Torre della Martella defensive tower in Corsica, hence the name.
Aldeburgh – The town of Aldeburgh has changed little in the 20th century and remains a delightful seaside resort. There are many interesting places in the town, the most famous being Moot Hall, a 16th-century building which now contains a small museum. The Hall was originally in the centre of the town but due to coastal erosion now stands on the sea front.

REFRESHMENTS:
There are numerous possibilities in Aldeburgh.

Walk 73   **ELMSETT**   5$\frac{1}{2}$m (9km)

Maps: OS Sheets Landranger 155; Pathfinder 1030.

A walk from a rural Suffolk village.

Start: At 059472, the lay-by close to St Peter's Church, Elmsett.

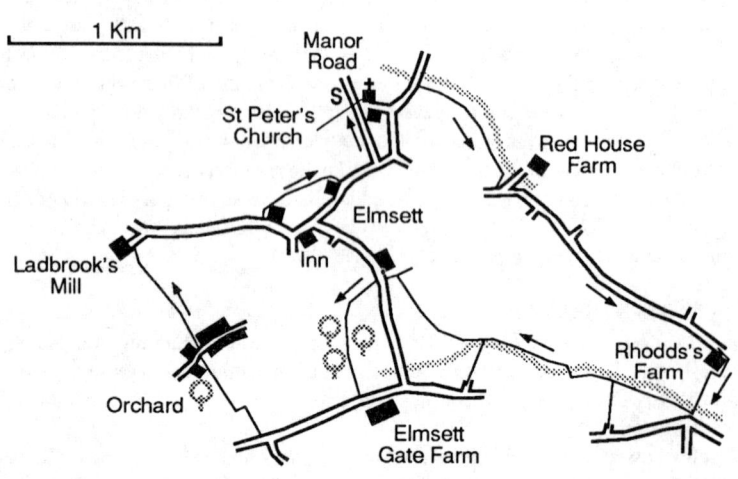

From the lay-by, walk back to St Peter's Church, opposite which is a plaque commemorating the **Tithe Wars**. Go into the churchyard and walk to the right of the church to reach a lane. Follow this, passing Church Farm on your right. At the end of the lane, turn left and go down to a bridge over a stream. Turn right before the bridge and follow the stream bank, continuing along the left-hand side of a large arable field to reach a metalled lane at its corner, opposite Red House Farm. Turn left and follow the lane for $\frac{3}{4}$ mile to reach Rhodds's Farm on the right.

Just past the farm buildings, take a waymarked path on the right, going around the back of the farm and then turning left to go downhill. At the bottom of the hill, go over a concrete bridge and then turn immediately right to follow the stream bank. At the end of the arable field on your left, continue into scrub land, soon reaching a concrete driveway leading to the water treatment works. Continue straight on, following the right-hand edge of a field and then going along a short cross-field path. At the field edge, turn left and walk around the field, soon crossing a small ditch. Just beyond the ditch, turn right and cross a sleeper bridge, and then go left to follow the edge of another field. Now maintain direction into the next field and across a trackway, then follow a cross-field path over two fields, heading for the corner of a house. At the corner, turn left to reach a metalled road. Cross the road and follow the track opposite along the right-hand edge of a field. In the corner of the field, cross a ditch and turn left to follow a path, soon going down the middle of a woodland strip and out on to a metalled lane.

Turn right and follow the lane to reach a road junction on your left. A few yards further on, take the path on your right, following it across a field and then over a sleeper bridge. Continue around the left-hand side of the next field to reach a stile into an orchard. Cross the stile and follow the right-hand edge of the orchard to reach a metalled lane. Turn right, but, after a few yards, turn left along a waymarked path heading towards Ladbrook's Mill in the distance. At the mill, turn right along a driveway, and then turn right again towards the centre of Elmsett. Just beyond the village sign, take the waymarked path on the left, following it behind the Old Rectory and continuing along the right-hand side of a field. Now go past the left-hand side of the village school to reach a metalled lane. Turn left, and then left again, going along Manor Road to return to St Peter's Church.

POINTS OF INTEREST:

Tithe Wars – During the 1920s and 1930s many farmers were still expected to pay tithes to the church, although very few of them were members of their local congregation. The tithes were based on pre-war corn values and with depressed prices in the 1920s many farmers refused to pay. As a result the 'Commissioners of Queen Ann's Bounty' seized livestock to auction them in order to redeem the tithe money. Civil unrest followed, this only being curtailed by the start of the World War II.

REFRESHMENTS:
The Rose & Crown, Elmsett.

Walk 74   BRANTHAM   5¹/₂m (9km)

Maps: OS Sheets Landranger 169; Pathfinder 1053.

A walk across pastures and down to the River Stour.

Start: At 102330, the southern end of the old bridge at Cattawade.

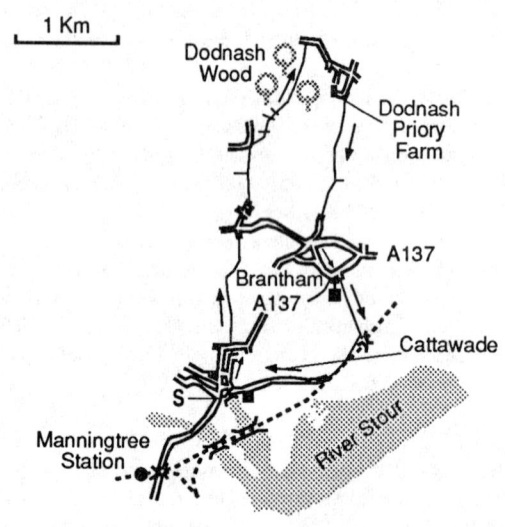

From the bridge, walk north along Cattawade Street and up to the main road (the A137). Cross the road, with care, and continue along the green lane opposite until you reach a metalled lane. Continue along the lane opposite (East End Lane), following it until it turns sharp left. There, continue straight ahead, going downhill along a cross-field path. Cross a ditch at the bottom of the hill and then go uphill to reach a metalled road at a corner. Take the path immediately on your right and go downhill, heading for distant plantation. Go through a hedge, across a pasture and then walk uphill to reach Dodnash Wood.

Go through the wood and then up a path towards the right-hand side of the next wood to reach a metalled road. Turn right along the road, passing a turning on the right and continuing to a crossroads. There, turn right along the driveway to Dodnash Priory Farm. Just in front of the farmhouse, turn left and follow the right-hand edge of a field to reach a stile. Cross the stile and head downhill, passing a pond on your left. Soon you will reach another stile: cross this stile into a meadow. Now bear slightly right to reach a gate on the far side, go through and bear left, uphill, to reach a stile. Cross the stile and bear right to follow a tree-lined track. Soon the track becomes a metalled lane (Gravel Pit Lane): continue along it to reach the main A137 again.

Cross the main road, again with care, and continue along the lane opposite (Church Lane), soon passing a road junction, on the right, and the old school house. Continue along the lane to reach St Michael's Church on the right. Just beyond the church, take a trackway on the right, following it down to the rectory. Pass the rectory along a wide track that soon goes downhill towards the railway. At the railway, turn right and follow a path to its right. Go past a sewage works, on your right, and then, just before the chemical works, bear right and then left to follow a path to a metalled lane. Continue along the lane to return to **Cattawade**. At the road junction, turn left to go over the old bridge, returning to the start of the walk.

POINTS OF INTEREST:
Cattawade – This is the site of the xylonite factory, built in 1887, which was the first purpose-built plastics factory in the country.

REFRESHMENTS:
The Crown, Cattawade.

CULFORD   5$\frac{1}{2}$m (9km)
or 9$\frac{1}{2}$m (15km)

Maps: OS Sheets Landranger 144; Pathfinder 963.
A circular walk through Culford and the King's Forest.
Start: At 815715, the car park at the picnic site, West Stow.

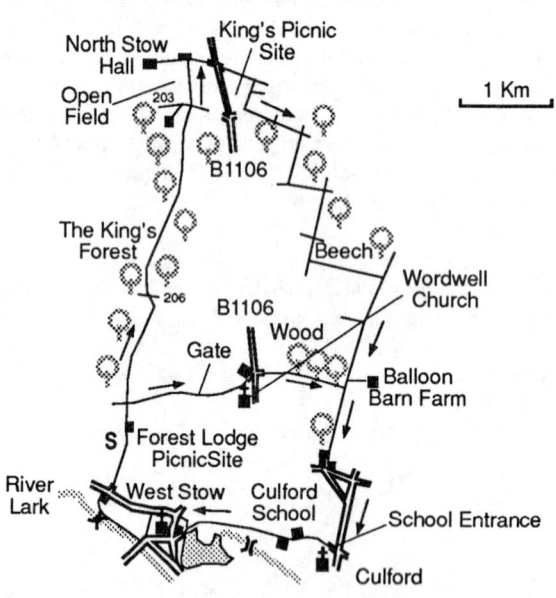

From the picnic site, turn left to follow the main driveway, passing the Forest Enterprise offices on your right. Continue on this main forest track (No. 205) to reach a junction of tracks.

The shorter walk turns right here, going along the edge of an open field to reach a wood. Go into the wood, then bear right to follow its right-hand edge to a metal gate. Go through the gate and bear left to follow a path across fields, heading towards Wordwell Church. When you reach a road (the B1106), cross with care, to the track opposite and follow this track across fields to the edge of a wood. Now maintain direction to reach a T-junction. Turn right to rejoin the longer walk opposite Balloon Barn Farm.

The longer walk continues straight on at the junction, following the track for about $^3/_4$ mile to reach another junction of main tracks. (The track to the left and right is No. 206.) Continue straight on along track No. 205 for a further $1^1/_4$ miles to reach another crossing track – No. 203. Again continue straight to reach some buildings, with North Stow Hall on your left. Turn right in front of the buildings and follow the track to a main road (the B1106). Cross, with care, and continue along the track opposite, with the King's picnic site on your right. After some 200 yards, take the track on the right, following the orange and blue waymarkers. Soon the track turns left: continue to follow it until you reach its junction with a major crossing track. Here, leave the orange and blue waymarkers, continuing straight ahead for another 200 yards to reach a birch plantation. Turn right and follow a path down to a T-junction. Turn left and, after some 200 yards, you will reach a major crossroads of tracks. Turn right and follow a track, passing a major junction of tracks and continuing to reach a crossing track with beech trees on your left and pines on your right. Turn left here and follow a path to reach a T-junction at the edge of the forest. Turn right and follow a path, passing arable fields on your right, to reach a copse opposite the track to Balloon Barn Farm. Here the shorter route – coming in from the right – is rejoined.

Continue along the path to reach a metalled road next to a road junction. Turn left, with care, and then bear left at the junction. After some 300 yards, turn right to follow a lane into Culford. Turn right into **Culford School**, following the driveway past the front of what was once a stately home. Continue along the driveway, passing a lake on the left, and then take a waymarked path on the right. Follow this path to reach a road opposite West Stow Church. Turn left and, after a few yards, turn right at a road junction. Follow the road down towards a bridge over the River Lark. Just before the bridge, turn right and follow the river bank to reach a weir. Bear right and follow a track into woodland, continuing through it to reach a road. Turn right, then left up a track. Now follow the track back to the picnic site.

POINTS OF INTEREST:
Culford School – The school was formerly Culford Hall, built by Sir Nicholas Bacon in 1591. In 1889 the estate passed to the Cadogan Family who rebuilt the Hall in its present style. In 1935 the estate was broken up and part of it became the King's Forest in commemoration of King George V's Jubilee.

REFRESHMENTS:
None on the route. The nearest is *The Cadogan Arms*, Ingham, a little way to the east.

Walk 77   **SHOTLEY AND THE TWO RIVERS**   6m (9¹/₂km)

Maps: OS Sheets Landranger 169; Pathfinder 1054.

A short walk through the three hamlets of Shotley.

Start: At 247336, the car park outside the Bristol Arms, Shotley
Gate.

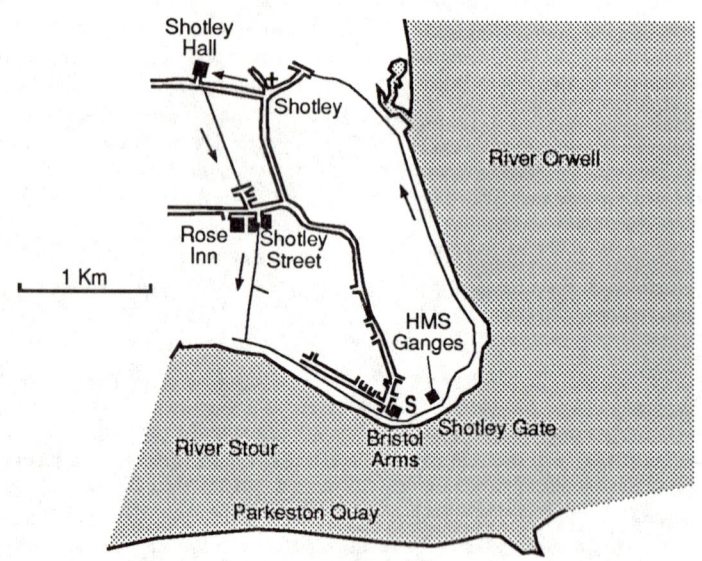

From the car park, follow the road into Shotley marina, with a view of Harwich, on
your right, and the cranes of Felixstowe dock straight ahead. Go to the right of the
boat park, passing the Shipwreck bar and restaurant, and bear left to follow the path
past the moorings. At the far end of the moorings the path continues straight ahead
along the sea wall. In the distance you can see Levington Marina.

Continue past the Harwich Harbour Board (HHB)/Ipswich Port Authority (IPA)
boundary marker and a footpath, on the left. Soon you pass saltmarsh on your right
and come to a hedge, on your left. Now follow the path down the bank and along the
left side of the hedge to reach a stile. Cross and continue along the left of the hedge,
heading towards **Shotley Church** in the distance. The path soon becomes a track which
bears left towards the church. Go past the church to reach a crossroads. Go straight

on, following the road to Shotley Hall, a very fine timber-framed house on the right. Turn left in front of the house, going down a waymarked green track between hedgerows. Just after an electricity pole the path goes right, and then left to continue down the left side of the adjacent field. Follow the path as it cuts across the bottom of the field, heading for a footbridge. Go over the bridge, turn right and then left up the side of a field, with a hedgerow on your left. Follow the path to a gap between houses and out into Garden Close. Turn left, and then right to follow Orwell View Road to the main road (the B1456). Turn right here for refreshments at the Rose Inn.

To continue the walk turn left at the junction and follow the road, with care, for about 80 yards. Now turn right, again with care, crossing the road to walk into Rose Farm. Go between the farm buildings and out into open fields. Continue along a track heading southwards towards an isolated house in the distance. At the house, keep straight on, heading towards Parkeston Quay in the distance, with the Felixstowe dock cranes on your left. At the bottom of the hill, turn left along another track following the river's edge. After 300 yards a path goes off to the right. This path along the foreshore can be followed back to Shotley Gate. However, this route is only recommended at low water. At all other times you should keep straight on along the edge of the field, going through a wood on the cliff top to reach a road (Stourside). Continue along the road but where it bears left, go along a path to reach another road (Estuary Road). Follow this road back to the main road and turn right to return to the car park.

POINTS OF INTEREST:
Shotley Church – St Mary's Church is noted for its lack of a tower or spire. Although from the outside the church looks somewhat patched up, inside it has some fine features including a hammerbeam roof. A church guide is available which details its history.
HMS Ganges – Until recently this was a Royal Naval training college. It is now a Suffolk Police training centre.

REFRESHMENTS:
The Bristol Arms, Shotley Gate.
The Shipwreck bar and restaurant, Shotley Marina.
The Rose Inn, Shotley Street.

LONG MELFORD   6m (9¹/₂km)
or 9m (14¹/₂km)

Maps: OS Sheets Landranger 155; Pathfinder 1029.
A walk around the edges of ancient woodland.
Start: At 865467, Holy Trinity Church, Long Melford.

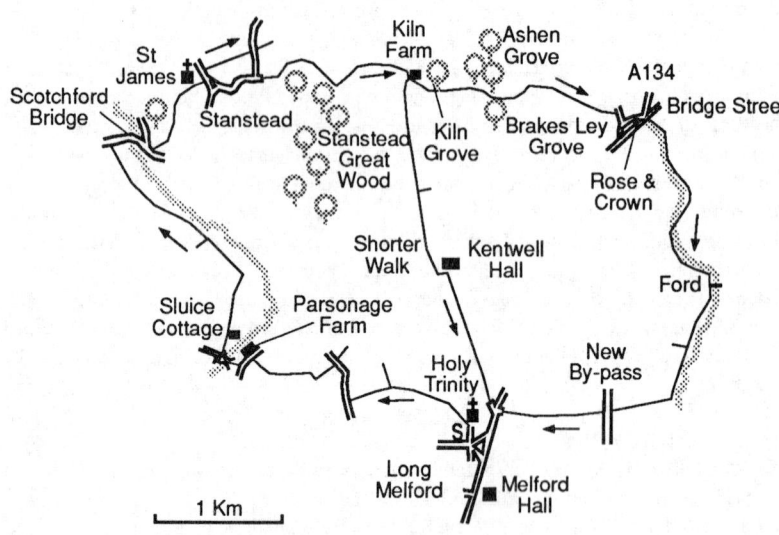

From the front of the church, walk along the left-hand side and go out of the churchyard through a bricked gateway. Continue straight on, ignoring waymark signs on your right, and follow the somewhat indistinct path around the right-hand edge of the field. Maintain direction, following the right-hand edges of further fields, to reach a metalled lane. Turn right, then, after 300 yards, turn left along a distinct path heading towards a distant oak tree. The path heads down to the corner of a small wood: turn right there, following a path to a lane by Parsonage Farm. Turn left, and then right to go to the left side of the farm passing some disused railway wagons. The path soon crosses a bridge over the River Glem and then runs to the left side of a small house (Sluice Cottage). Continue on to reach a ditch and a junction of paths. Turn left and walk with the ditch on your right. After about a mile the path joins a metalled lane at Scotchford Bridge.

Turn right to cross the bridge and continue along the lane to reach a T-junction. Turn right, and then left, to follow a path up brick steps and along the right-hand side of Scotchford Wood. Continue along the path to reach the back of St James's Church, Stanstead. From the front of the church, turn left, and then right, to follow a path between houses. Follow the path to an open field, continuing along it down to a metalled lane. Turn right. After 200 yards, turn left to follow a track, keeping woodland (Stanstead Great Wood) on your right. Soon the path leaves the wood and bears to the right, heading towards Kiln Farm. Just passed Kiln Farm there is a junction of tracks.

The shorter route keeps straight ahead here, going down a track past Kentwell Hall and then along an avenue of lime trees to reach the main entrance where the longer route is rejoined.

The longer walk turns left at the junction of tracks, following the somewhat muddy bridleway past Kiln Grove and Ashen Grove, on the left, and then Brakes Ley Grove, on the right. At the corner of the wood, keep straight ahead across an open field, going to the end of a remnant hedge. Turn left and then, soon, right to cross an open field. Continue to reach the houses at Bridge Street. At the metalled road turn right, and then left to pass around the back of houses. Now bear right to reach the main road (the A134) at the Rose and Crown. Cross the road, with care, and follow the lane opposite past Ford Hall. Now go down the track on the right. At first this long track keeps to the left of the stream, then changes sides to run along the right-hand side of the stream. After about a mile you will reach a ford. Do not cross; instead, turn right, and then left just past a World War II pill box. Continue along the left-hand edge of the field. Eventually the path turns sharp right and leads up to the new bypass. Cross, with care, and continue along the concrete driveway opposite, following it to the entrance to **Kentwell Hall** where the shorter route is rejoined.

Go through the entrance and take the path on the left heading towards the back of Holy Trinity Church. Just past the cemetery, turn left, cross a paddock and then turn left again to return to the church and the start of the walk in **Long Melford**.

POINTS OF INTEREST:

Kentwell Hall – The Hall was built in the mid-16th century by the Clopton family.
Long Melford – This is one of Suffolk's loveliest villages. Holy Trinity Church is considered by many to be the finest in the county. Melford Hall, a turreted brick Tudor mansion, is owned by the National Trust.

REFRESHMENTS:

The Rose and Crown, Bridge Street, Long Melford.
There are also other possibilities in Long Melford.

Walk 80   FELSHAM AND BRADFIELD WOODS   6m (9¹/₂km)

Maps: OS Sheets Landranger 155; Pathfinder 1006.

A walk through ancient coppiced woodland.

Start: At 935580, the Bradfield Woods National Nature Reserve car park.

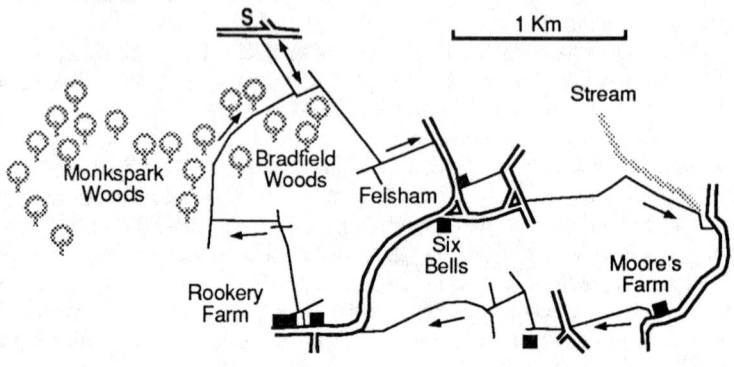

From the car park, follow the main track into the woods for about 100 yards to reach an opening. There, take the path to the left, following red waymarkers. The path soon reaches a public right of way: turn right. At the next junction, turn left and then, after a few yards, left again over a small bridge to exit the Nature Reserve. Follow the edge of the field to the bottom of the hill and turn left, following the path to a road. Turn right along the road and then left on to a waymarked path just past a cottage on the left. The path soon reaches another road: turn right into Felsham village.

At the village green – the Six Bells is just ahead here – by the water pump, take the path on the left, following the left-hand edge of a field. Now follow the waymarked path around the edges of several fields, passing a lake, on the left, to reach a road. Turn right up the road for some 90 yards, then, just past **Moore's Farm**, turn right, and very soon left, to go down the right-hand side of a field. At the bottom of the slight hill, go through the hedge, cross a sleeper bridge and then go uphill, turning right, and then left, to reach a metalled road. Cross the road and take the path opposite, bearing right across the open field. Continue past Brooke's Farm and then bear right, heading towards **Felsham Church** in the distance.

Near the bottom of the hill, take the path on the left, crossing a field towards its far corner, walking parallel to a stream on your right. Keep straight on, now with a hedgerow on your right, and where another path, from the left, joins your path, turn right through a gap in the hedge into the adjacent field. Bear left and cross to the far side of the field, then turn left to follow the right-hand bank of a ditch to a metalled lane. Turn left along the lane. Just after a turning on the left, take a waymarked path on the right, beside a cottage. Just behind the cottage the path divides: take the left-hand path into a field and then go right to follow the path to a small wood. Keep to the right-hand side of the wood, following the path across an open field. After some 100 yards take a path on the left (this may not be waymarked), following it to the corner of Monkspark Woods. Turn right and follow the edge of the woods to another corner. Now continue straight on into **Bradfield Woods**. In the wood, follow the blue waymarkers to return to the main car park.

POINTS OF INTEREST:

Moore's Farm – The barn beside the road at Moore's Farm was decorated by its previous owner with paintings of places he had visited and now is an unusual attraction for visitors to the area.

Felsham Church – This 14th-century church is dedicated to St Peter. The west tower contains six bells, made in the 17th century, these giving their name to the public house opposite.

Bradfield Woods – This is one of the oldest continually coppiced woodlands in England and has recently been designated a National Nature Reserve.

REFRESHMENTS:

The Six Bells, Felsham.

Walk 81   **LAXFIELD**   6m ($9\frac{1}{2}$km)

Maps: OS Sheets Landranger 156; Pathfinder 965.

A pleasant walk around the village of Laxfield.

Start: At 296725, the lay-by outside the King's Head, Laxfield.

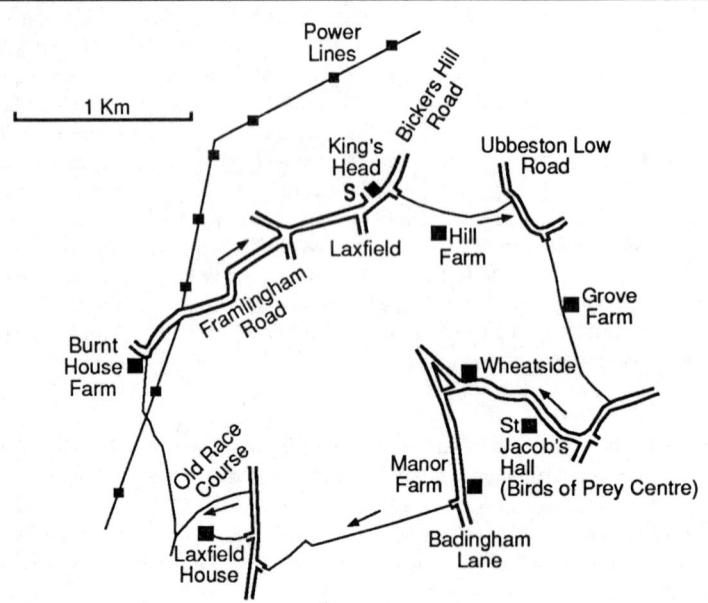

From the lay-by go back to the road junction with Bickers Hill Road and turn left. After some 100 yards, turn right along a farm track with hedgerows on either side. Where the track turns right to go to Hill Farm, keep straight on along a path which soon enters an arable field. Here a permissive path has been created along the right-hand field edge, going downhill towards a distant cottage. From the back of the cottage, turn left and then, soon, right to reach a metalled road (Ubbeston Low Road).

Turn right past the cottage and, soon, right again to follow a track up to Grove Farm. Pass to the right-hand side of the farmhouse and then go straight on, across an arable field to reach the corner of an adjacent field. Cross a small sleeper bridge and continue around the left-hand edge of the field. Continue along the edge of the field, passing a small pond, and staying close to the left-hand side of the next field to reach another sleeper bridge. Cross and continue to a metalled lane. Turn right along the lane, and bear right at a road junction. Go past St Jacob's Hall Birds of Prey Centre, on your left, continuing to the next road junction, opposite a bungalow (Wheatside) on the right. Turn left and, after 100 yards, left again along Badingham Lane. Follow the lane to Manor Farm, on the left, and there take the waymarked track on the right, opposite the farm house.

Follow this well-defined track for almost a mile to reach the Dennington Road. Turn right along the road, passing the driveway of Laxfield House. Continue for a further 200 yards and then take a waymarked path on the left. Go down the left-hand side of a field, with a hedgerow on your left, to reach a stile in the corner. Cross and continue along the left-hand side of the next field to reach a metal gate. Go into the next field and bear slightly left, heading for a three-fingered waymarker in the top left corner.

Now take the path on your right, continuing, between hedgerows, along the 'Old Race Course'. The track soon opens out into an arable field: turn right and follow the edge of the field to a corner. Go through a gap in the hedge and walk straight across an open field, heading for the right-hand side of the distant buildings (Burnt House). Go down the right-hand side of the farm buildings to reach Framlingham Road. Turn right, along the road, heading back to **Laxfield**. At the war memorial, turn right along the High Street passing the Baptist Chapel, on the left, and the **Guildhall Museum**, on the right. Turn left past the old Royal Oak (now closed), and left again to return to the King's Head and the lay-by start point.

POINTS OF INTEREST:
Laxfield – The village's main claim to fame is that it was the birthplace of William Dowsing the Puritan zealot. In 1643 he was appointed 'Parliamentary Visitor to the Churches of Suffolk' and spared no time in destroying many of the medieval icons and artefacts from the surrounding churches.
Guildhall Museum – This interesting museum is open from 2-5pm on Saturdays, Sundays and Bank Holidays during the summer.

REFRESHMENTS:
The King's Head, Laxfield (also known as *Low House*).
Refreshments are also available at the St Jacob's Hall Birds of Prey Centre on the route.

Walk 82   HOXNE AND THE ROMAN TREASURE   6m (9½km)

Maps: OS Sheets Landranger 156; Pathfinder 964.

A walk around the historic village of Hoxne.

Start: At 181773, the Village Green, Hoxne.

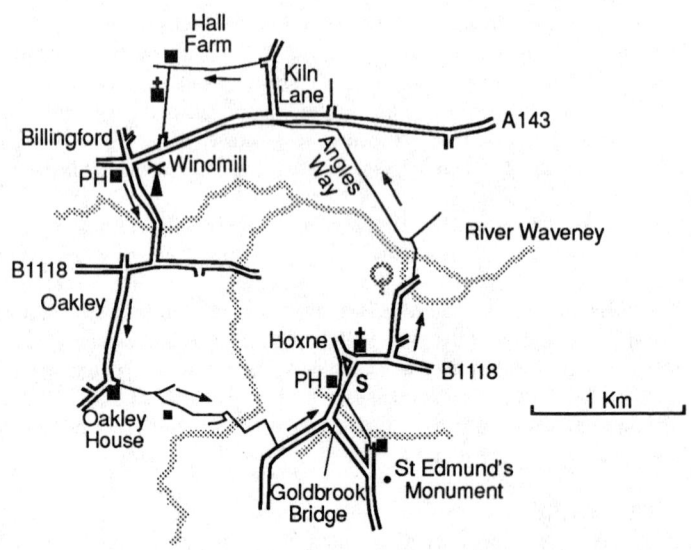

From the right-hand corner of the Village Green, head north along the lane towards the church. At a road junction, turn right, with care, and, after a few yards, turn left to go down Water Mill Lane. Where the lane turns right, keep straight on, heading down to a bridge over the River Waveney. Turn left and follow the path along the bank of the river to reach a second bridge and weir. Cross this bridge and turn left towards a stile, ignoring the fisherman's stile near the river. Go over the stile and bear left to follow the Angles Way around the left-hand edge of the field. Where the path leaves the river, go up to the next corner and then keep straight on into the adjacent field. Now follow the cross-field path to meet the busy A143 road. Turn left and, with great care, follow the road for some 400 yards to reach a road on the right. Take this (Kiln Lane), following it for about 300 yards before turning left along a gravel driveway. Follow the driveway to reach a lane at Hall Farm. Turn left and follow the lane, passing Billingford Church on the right. Where the lane joins the main road (the A143) turn right, again with care, and follow the road towards the Three Horseshoes. Just before the public house, turn left and follow a lane, passing Billingford Wind Mill on your left. Cross a bridge over the River Waveney and continue to reach another main road (the B1118).

Turn right, with care, and then, after some 300 yards, turn left along the road to Brome Street. Just before reaching Oakley House, on your left, turn left along a private driveway, soon reaching a junction of tracks. Take the right-hand track, going past a small cottage on the right. Continue along the track, passing a house and a lake on your right, and then, where the track turns sharp right, continue straight on along a path. The path becomes narrower and leads down to a bridge over the River Dove. Cross the bridge and follow the path along an avenue of poplar trees. At the end of the avenue, turn right and follow the edge of the field to a metalled lane. Turn left and follow the lane down to a road junction. Turn right to cross **Goldbrook Bridge**, soon passing St Edmund's Hall on the right. Just past some cottages, on the left, you will reach the end of a driveway: on the left here, in the middle of the field, you can see the **monument** to King Edmund. Turn left down the driveway and go to the left-hand side of a barn, continuing to reach a small bridge. Cross the bridge and follow the path beyond back to the Village Green in **Hoxne**, reaching it opposite the Swan.

POINTS OF INTEREST:

Goldbrook Bridge/Monument – This is the bridge where King Edmund was hiding before being discovered and killed by the Danes in 870AD. The monument commemorates the king's death.

Hoxne – The village is famous for the Hoxne Treasure, which has been called the greatest Roman treasure ever to have been discovered in this country. It consists of 14,870 coins and 200 objects, all gold and silver. The hoard was found by chance in November 1992 by Mr Eric Lawes while searching in a field for a friend's hammer. He reported it at once to the Suffolk Archaeological Unit, who carefully excavated the treasure, removing it in sections. Detailed examination and recording were completed by staff at the British Museum. The early involvement of the archaeologists was crucial to the recovery of many small fragments of silver and textile, and provided evidence of the way in which the hoard was buried. The treasure is now housed in the British Museum.

REFRESHMENTS:
The Swan, Hoxne.
The Three Horseshoes, Billingford.

Walk 83   COVEHITHE   6m (9½km)

Maps: OS Sheets Landranger 156; Pathfinder 946.

A walk along country lanes and eroding shoreline.

Start: At 529820, the end of the lane that goes past St Andrew's Church.

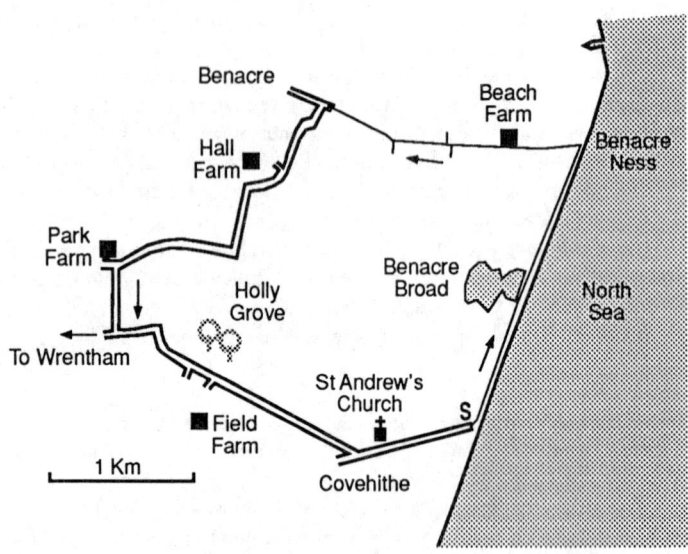

From the end of the lane, walk to the edge of the cliff and turn left along a path. (The cliff edge along this part of the coast is very unstable and care should be taken not to walk too near to the edge.) Follow this concessionary path along the top of the cliff, soon reaching the edge of Benacre National Nature Reserve.

Now follow a path down on to the sandy bar between Benacre Broad and the sea. At the end of the bar the path goes uphill to the cliff top again: continue along the path to reach a metalled lane at Benacre Ness. Turn left along the lane, following it to reach a gate and stile across the lane, by the entrance to Beach Farm. Cross the stile and continue along the lane, heading towards Benacre Church in the distance, to reach a metalled lane at a bend. Turn left and follow the lane, soon passing Hall Farm on your right. Continue along the lane to reach Park Farm, also on your right. Just past the farm, turn sharp left and follow a lane to its T-junction with a road. Turn left and follow the road, soon passing Holly Grove, on your left, and the entrance to Field Farm, on your right.

When the road reaches a junction, bear left to follow the lane past St Andrew's Church, **Covehithe**, on your left, continuing to reach the starting point.

POINTS OF INTEREST:

Covehithe – Now only a church and a few houses, this was once a thriving fishing community of about 300 people. The Church of St Andrew was built in 1459 and was always too big for the congregation. In 1672 the nave and chancel were demolished to provide building material for the now smaller church.

The coast near the village here has always been subject to erosion and is now eroding by as much as 3 metres (10 feet) a year.

REFRESHMENTS:

There are no refreshments en route or at Covehithe, the nearest being at Wrentham, a mile or so to the west.

Walk 84   **WESTLETON**   6m (9¹/₂km)
Maps: OS Sheets Landranger 156; Pathfinder 987.
A walk along the old course of the River Minsmere.
Start: At 441691, beside the village pond, Westleton.

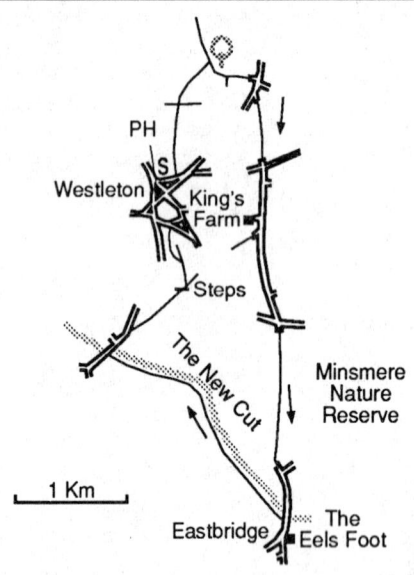

From the village pond, near the White Horse, follow the left-hand edge of the village green and turn left along a footpath on its left-hand side. Continue along this path until it reaches an open field. Now follow a cross-field path and then go along the left-hand side of an open field. Soon you will come to cross-paths: continue ahead, keeping to the left-hand field edge. At the end of the field, cross a sleeper bridge into the adjacent field and bear right across an indistinct cross-field path heading for a distant waymarker next to a copse (Loompit).

At the copse, turn right and follow a track to a metalled lane. Turn right and, after a few yards, you will reach a footpath and trackway on your left. Ignore this track, but take the next track on the left a few yards further along the road. Follow this track, initially through woodland and then across heathland to reach a metalled lane at a T-junction. Cross and follow the lane opposite, passing King's Farm on the right and continuing down to another junction. Keep straight on, following a track opposite down the side of the **Minsmere Nature Reserve.** When you come to a metalled lane, continue straight on to reach a bridge over the newly formed **River Minsmere.**

Cross the bridge and turn right to follow the bank of the river to reach a bridge and metalled road. Turn right and follow the road, passing a turning on your left, towards **Westleton.** After a few yards you will reach a bend: turn right and follow a trackway, soon passing a treatment works on your right. Continue along the track to reach some steps cut into a bank on the left. Go up the steps and follow a path across a disused sand pit. Now bear right to follow the path to a metalled lane. Cross the lane and go along a track opposite to reach a second lane. Turn left and follow this lane back into Westleton. Cross the main village road and head back to the village pond and the end of the walk.

POINTS OF INTEREST:
Minsmere Nature Reserve – The Reserve was purchased by the RSPB in 1947 from the Ogilvie family. It is famous for the reintroduction of avocets into Britain. The Reserve is still growing in size and now represents a classic area of managed heathland that used to exist all along the Sandlings.

River Minsmere – The original river meandered through the marshes from Middleton to the sea, but in 1813 the Minsmere Levels Drainage Trust cut a new straight channel, effectively draining the surrounding area and forming wet grazing meadows. The course of the old river can still be detected in places.

Westleton – The village was recorded in the Domesday Book as *Westlede's Tun* after a Norse settler called Vestildhi. Around the village are 18 limes trees planted to commemorate the 18 villagers who gave their lives during World War I.

REFRESHMENTS:
The Crown, Westleton.
The White Horse, Westleton.
The Eel's Foot, Eastbridge.

Walk 85   **PLAYFORD AND THE FYNN VALLEY** $6^1/_4$m (10km)

Maps: OS Sheets Landranger 169; Pathfinder 1031.

A circular walk around the Fynn valley.

Start: At 229478, the car park outside the Admiral's Head, Great Bealings.

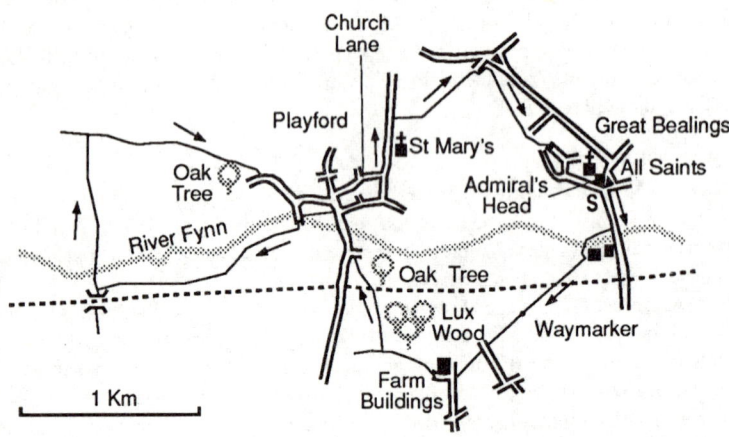

From the car park, turn right and go downhill towards the River Fynn. Just before the river, turn right and follow the river bank to a small bridge. Cross the river and follow the path beyond past a barn, on your left. Now bear right across a field towards a level crossing. Cross the railway, with care, and bear right across an arable field towards a waymarker at the top of the hill. Continue roughly in the same direction across another arable field heading for the distant farm buildings, not the house to the right. At the farm, go straight on, through buildings, and then bear right along a track just before an open field. Follow this track past a row of horse chestnut trees, on your right, and then turn right along a path at the corner of Lux Wood.

Follow the path down the left side of the wood and across an arable field, walking towards a distant level crossing and heading to the left of an oak tree. Cross the level crossing, with care, and walk across the field beyond. Now turn left along a track and then right along a metalled road. Follow the road downhill and over the River Fynn, then turn left into a wood just opposite a road junction. Walk through the wood to reach a bridge. Turn left along a track and then right into a field, following its left edge. Now ignore the first path, but take the second path on the left into a wood. Follow the path through the wood, with the railway on your left. The path eventually joins a track: turn right and head for a bridge over the river. Cross and go uphill, passing a disused quarry on your left. At the top of the hill, just before the track turns left, take a path on the right. Follow the path to where it turns left, and there keep straight on through a gap in the hedge and follow the left side of the field beyond. At the corner of the field, bear right and head for a distant oak tree. From the oak tree, follow the track past woodland, on your right, and then go down a sandy lane. At the bottom of the slope, turn left and follow the lane into Playford. Go over the cross-roads and along Church Lane to reach **St Mary's Church**.

Turn left at the church and walk uphill. Take the next footpath on the right, just past a farm building, and, after some 300 yards, follow the path as it bears left across a field towards a wood. Waymarkers should help you here. Go along the edge of the field, with the wood on your left, and cross a stile in the corner. Keep straight on, now walking between two fences, until you reach the top of the hill. Here the path goes right, then left to follow the left edge of a field. In the corner of the field, turn sharp right and follow a cross-field path, walking parallel with the road and heading towards the right-hand end of distant cottages. The path passes to the right of the cottages, then leads into Michael's Mount (Close). Turn left, and then right at the junction with Richard's Drive. Now go left along Sandy Lane to return to the Admiral's Head and car park.

POINTS OF INTEREST:
St Mary's Church – A 'Brief History and Guide' is available in both St Mary's Church, Playford and All Saints Church, Great Bealings. The guide is worth obtaining for the fascinating insight into the history of both these fine churches.

REFRESHMENTS:
The Admiral's Head, Great Bealings.
The village stores in Playford is also a useful source of refreshments.

Walk 86   HAVERHILL AND KEDINGTON   6¼m (10km)

Maps: OS Sheets Landranger 154; Pathfinder 1028.

A walk along the Stour valley to Kedington.

Start: At 685448, the East Town Park car park, off Coupals Road, Haverhill.

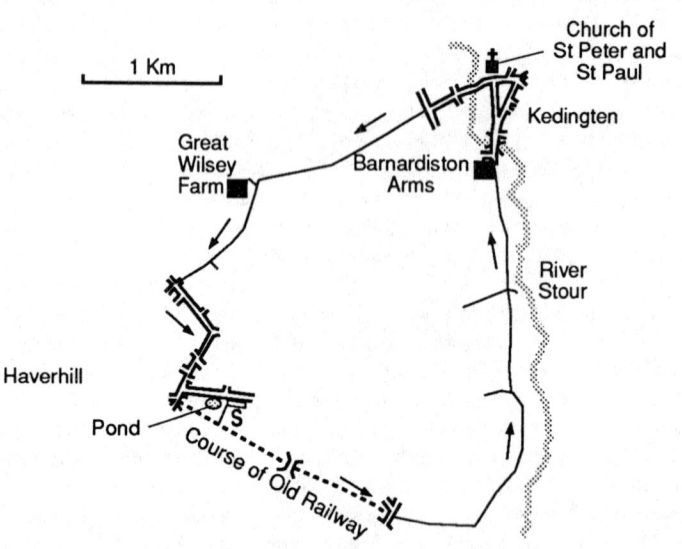

From the car park, go through a gate into the adjacent meadow and bear right, passing a pond on your right. Go over a bridge and then up steps to reach a disused railway. Turn left and follow the embankment, passing some houses on the right. (The stile on your right leads to the Red Lion, Sturmer).

Continue along the embankment for a further 800 yards to reach a road. Turn left by a telephone kiosk and then, after a few paces, turn right along a track. Soon you will reach an open field: follow the field's right-hand edge, then keep to the main path as it again follows the old railway. Soon the path veers left taking you past the low lying meadows at the junction of the Stour Brook and the River Stour. Keep straight on along the right-hand side of the field, eventually reaching a gravel path. Follow this to the corner of a metalled lane. Now keep straight on to reach the main road in the village of Kedington (pronounced Ketton), with the **Barnardiston Arms** to your left.

Turn right, crossing a bridge over the river. Now, just past a disused garage on your left, turn left along an avenue of lime trees to reach a road opposite the **Church of St Peter and St Paul**. Turn left and follow the road down to the river, reaching it by a watermill on the right. Continue along the road, soon reaching a T-junction. Turn left, and then right, opposite a telephone kiosk, on to a track. Where the track turns left, keep straight on up the hill ahead, crossing a very large open field. Continue to Great Wilsey Farm, turning left there to pass some fuel tanks. Continue down a track and, just past a plantation on your left, bear right at a junction of tracks. Continue to a T-junction opposite a housing development on the outskirts of Haverhill. Turn left and follow the road down, passing Coupals Road to reach a bridge over the Stour Brook. Just before the bridge, turn left along the disused railway embankment and then, after some 100 yards, go left again down steps to return to the car park.

POINTS OF INTEREST:

Barnardiston Arms – The name derives from one of the main families in the district, the Barnardistons who were severe Puritans. It is said that the name 'Roundhead' was first bestowed on Samuel Barnardiston whose short-cropped hair provoked the comment from Queen Henrietta 'what a handsome roundhead is there'.

The Church of St Peter and St Paul – This fine church at Kedington dates from the 13th century and contains many noteworthy features including a 16th-century parish chest and a canopied pew with separate sections for men and women.

REFRESHMENTS:

The Barnardiston Arms, Kedington.
The White Horse, Kedington.
The Red Lion, Sturmer.
Ketton Tea Rooms, Kedington.

Maps: OS Sheets Landranger 156; Pathfinder 1008.

A walk across Snape Warren to Friston.

Start: At 392575, the car park at Snape Maltings.

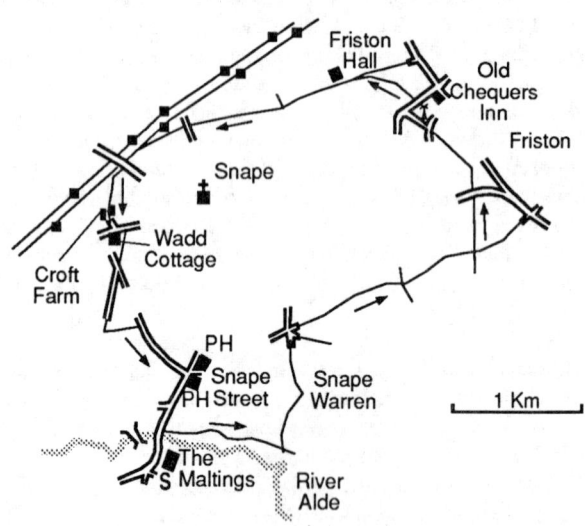

From the car park go out to the main road and turn right to cross the bridge over the River Alde. Once across the bridge, turn right just in front of a cottage and right again to go on to the river wall. Turn left to follow the river wall for some 900 yards to reach the woodland of Snape Warren. Beware of adders along the river wall and on the heath in summer.

As you enter the wood, turn left to follow a well-defined track, soon reaching heathland on your right. Continue along the track to reach a bend on a metalled lane. Turn right and take the left-hand of two tracks, passing to the left-hand side of a white cottage. Continue along this sandy track, passing a pink cottage on the right. Just after the cottage you will reach a junction of tracks: go straight on for another 600 yards to reach a point where a track goes off to the right. Turn left here and follow an unmarked path along the left-hand edge of a field, with hedgerow on your left. Follow the path

164

to a waymarker on the Aldeburgh Road. Cross the road and the field opposite, heading towards a windmill in the distance. At the opposite side of the field, bear left to follow the field edge to the left-hand corner where a path leads off through the gorse to reach a metalled lane at a T-junction. Cross the lane and maintain direction up the lane opposite to reach another junction. Turn right and follow the lane past a windmill, on your right. (Keep straight on into Friston to visit the Old Chequers Inn).

Now turn left, just before some terraced houses, along a path, going over a stile and across an open field, bearing left towards the distant hedgerow. Go through the hedgerow and continue on to reach a concrete track. Bear left and follow the track past Friston Hall, on your right. Continue along the track, passing a house on your right. Now, where the track turns right, bear slightly left to follow a well-defined track across open fields. Follow this track for some 700 yards to reach a metalled lane. Cross the lane and continue along another track, with electricity pylons on your right, heading down to reach a road. Cross the road and follow the track opposite to Croft Farm.

Go through the farm and, where the path divides, take the left-hand branch, following it to reach a metalled lane opposite a bungalow (Wadd Cottage). Turn left, and then right, just past the bungalow. Cross the stile to the left of the bungalow and follow the marked path across an arable field, heading down to a distant cottage. Pass to the right of this cottage, going along a small lane which soon peters out into a track. At the end of the track, turn left and go up a hill to the right of a large garden. At the top of the hill you will reach a metalled lane: turn right and follow the lane down to reach Snape Street opposite the Crown. Turn right and follow the road back across the River Alde to return to the car park at **Snape Maltings**.

POINTS OF INTEREST:

Snape Maltings – Set on the banks of the River Alde, this unique collection of 19th-century maltings includes many interesting shops and galleries. The concert hall and the Britten-Pears School for Advanced Musical Studies are home to the Aldeburgh Festival of Music and Arts as well as a year round programme of concerts and master classes.

REFRESHMENTS:
Ye Old Plough and Sail, Snape Maltings.
The Old Chequers Inn, Friston.
The Golden Key, Snape Street.
The Crown, Snape Street.

Walk 88 MOULTON, DALHAM AND GAZELEY $6\frac{1}{2}$m ($10\frac{1}{2}$km)

Maps: OS Sheets Landranger 154; Pathfinder 983.

A walk around the three villages.

Start: At 699641, the lay-by opposite St Peter's Church, Moulton.

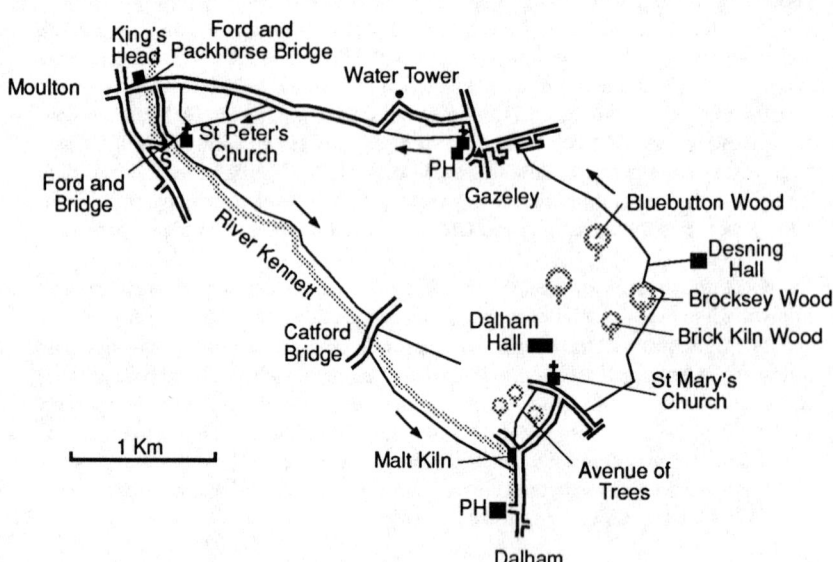

From the lay-by, follow a gravel track along the left-hand bank of the River Kennett, eventually reaching a metalled lane. Turn right, cross Catford Bridge and, after a further 100 yards, turn left along a footpath, following it along the other bank of the river to reach a stile and bridge. Cross and turn right to follow the lane into Dalham for refreshments.

To continue the walk turn left along the lane, passing an old malt kiln on your left. Just beyond a road junction, take the footpath on the left, following the avenue of trees to reach a road at St Mary's Church. **Dalham Hall**, the one-time home of Wellington, is situated just behind the church.

Turn right and follow the road past a junction, on your right, continuing to the top of a slight hill. There, take the footpath on the left, walking along the edge of a wood. At the end of the wood, continue to Brick Kiln Wood, now walking with woodland on your left and an arable field on your right. At the end of the field, turn left to go into Blocksey Wood. Follow the waymarked path around both Blocksey Wood and, next, Bluebutton Wood.

. Soon the path comes out into an arable field: turn left and head towards Gazeley Church in the distance. The path crosses several fields and then passes between houses to reach a close. Bear left and follow waymarkers past Tithe Close to reach a metalled lane. Turn left and walk down to a T-junction. Turn right to pass in front of All Saint's Church, Gazeley, and then take the path down the right-hand side of the churchyard. Continue along this path, soon going along a hedge-lined track and passing Gazeley Stud on your right.

Where the track meets the Moulton Road, turn left and follow the road for some 800 yards to reach a path going off to the left. Turn left here, then bear right to follow the path across an arable field. Go over a stile and continue down to the edge of a wood. Cross another stile and continue heading downhill to reach a stile at the back of St Peter's Church, Moulton. If you want refreshments, turn right here and then left at the main road, passing the **packhorse bridge** to reach the Kings Head.

To continue the walk, go over the stile and walk past the church, on your left. Continue along the driveway to return to the start of the walk.

POINTS OF INTEREST:
Dalham Hall – The Hall was built in 1704 for Bishop Symon Patrick of Ely. The Duke of Wellington lived here for some time and later it was bought by Cecil Rhodes although he never actually lived there.
Packhorse bridge – The bridge in Moulton is 15th-century, its low parapet walls designed to enable the horses' packs to swing clear.

REFRESHMENTS:
The King's Head, Moulton.
The Affleck Arms, Dalham.
The Chequers, Gazeley.

Walk 89   HADLEIGH: TOWN AND AROUND   7m (11km)

Maps: OS Sheets Landranger 155; Pathfinder 1030.

A walk through Bullocky Fen and along a disused railway track.

Start: At 027426, the car park behind Hadleigh High Street.

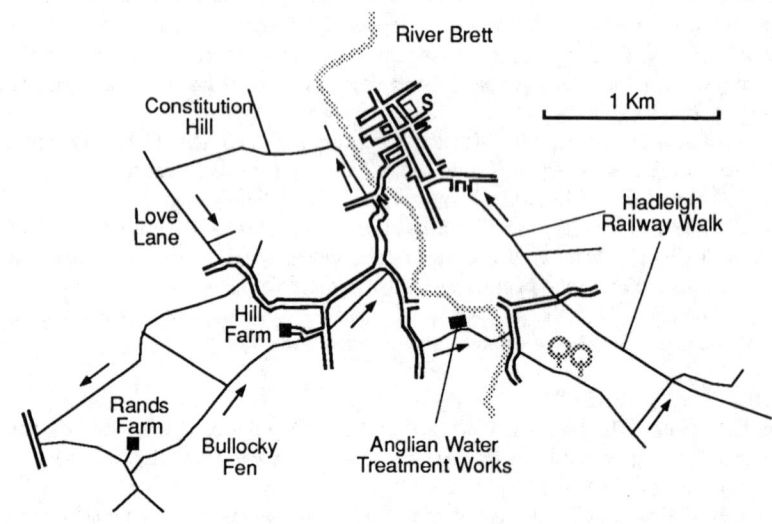

From the car park exit, follow the sign to High Street. Turn left and then take the second turning right, down Duke Street, to reach Toppesfield bridge. Cross the bridge and turn right along the riverside walk. Take the next waymarked path on the left, signposted to Broom Hill, and follow the path out of the wood and over a stile. Now go left, following the edge of a field to reach the Broom Hill Nature Reserve.

Do not enter the reserve: instead, follow the left-hand path up the edge of the Reserve, then continue up Constitution Hill, ignoring a path on the right. Continue along the edge of two fields to reach a green lane (Love Lane). Turn left and follow the lane down to a metalled road, ignoring a track on the left. Turn left along the road and then go right at the next footpath sign. Follow this path along the edge of two fields, then bear left to reach a stile. Cross the stile and head for a bridge over a stream. Now maintain direction, going uphill to reach another stile. Maintain direction again, crossing a large arable field towards a signpost at the edge of a road. Turn left along the road for a few yards, then go left again down the green lane leading to Rands Farm.

At the metalled lane, turn left into the farm, keeping to right-hand side of the farmyard and then continuing along a waymarked green lane into Bullocky Fen. Follow the path through the fen, passing a fishing lake, then turn left along a path leading to a stile and a field. Go uphill, following a headland path on the left towards Hill Farm. Follow a waymarked detour to bypass the farm, following the path to reach a metalled lane on a bend. Keep straight on, following the lane down to a T-junction. Cross to the footpath opposite. The footpath bears slightly left to reach the distant corner of a field and then goes down to a metalled road: turn right along the road, passing a driveway on the left. Now take the next waymarked path on the left, heading towards the Anglian Water treatment works.

Cross two stiles and a bridge over the River Brett, then cross a pasture to reach a stile on to the main road. Turn right, with care, and, after about 100 yards, take a path on the left by an outbuilding. The path leads diagonally across a small field into a wood. Walk through the wood and a new plantation to reach an open field. Follow a path uphill and then right along the crest of the hill. After about 500 yards, turn left at a waymarker and head towards the distant trees, eventually climbing a bank to reach a disused railway track. From here Hadleigh Station is waymarked as one mile away. Turn left and follow the track to the disused Station. There, turn left along a metalled road, and then right down Magdallen Road to return to the car park in **Hadleigh**.

POINTS OF INTEREST:
Hadleigh – This is an old Suffolk wool town and has many fine timber framed buildings. Information on places of interest to visit can be found at the Tourist Information Office.

REFRESHMENTS:
There are several inns in Hadleigh, many providing coffee and tea as well as lunches. There is also an excellent coffee shop.

Walk 90 TUNSTALL FOREST AND THE RIVER ALDE 7m (11km)
Maps: OS Sheets Landranger 156; Pathfinder 1008 and 1009.
A circular walk with open heath, forest and river edge.
Start: At 382565, the car park on Blaxhall Common, Snape.

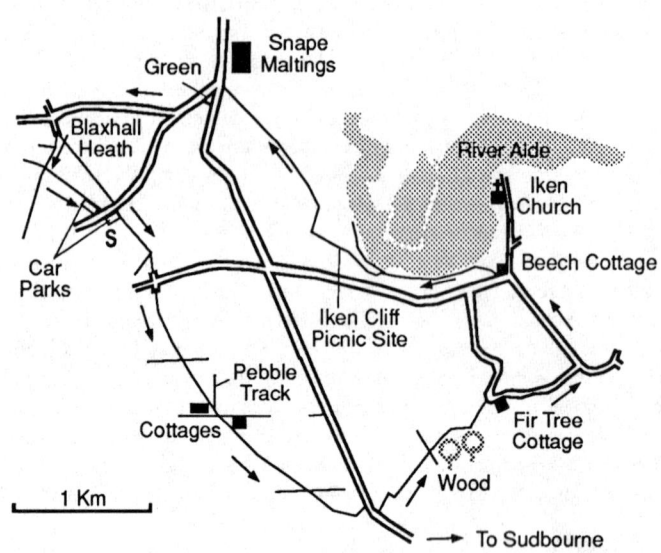

From the car park, on the eastern side of the Tunstall/Snape Road, head south-eastwards along a well-defined track through gorse and bracken. Maintain direction to reach a metalled road. Cross and continue to reach a crossing of tracks by some cottages. Now go straight on, passing a cottage on your left, and following the yellow forest waymarkers. The path gets narrower and meanders somewhat before reaching the Snape to Sudbourne road. Cross the road and follow the path opposite along the left-hand edge of a field. At a junction with a track, keep straight on, following the right-hand side of a field, with woodland on your right. Soon you will meet a road: turn right, passing Fir Tree Cottage. Soon, turn left to follow the road towards **Iken Church**, which is reached by taking a detour to the right at the next road junction.

The route bears left, passing Church Cottage, on the left. Now take the next footpath on the right, just past Beech Cottage. The path soon drops down to the side of the river and continues along the water's edge. After about 200 yards, take a path on the left, between two fences just before a cottage. The path goes up steps and around a cottage to reach a junction with another track. Turn right and follow the track towards Snape. Cross another track and continue to the Ikencliff picnic site. The path continues along the edge of the car park, then goes across the marsh to reach the Snape Road. Turn right here if you wish to visit the **Snape Maltings**.

To continue the walk, cross the road and green, and turn left along the road to Tunstall. After 200 yards, take a right fork along the road to Blaxhall. Follow this road until to reach a road junction on the right. Take the path opposite the road junction on to **Blaxhall Heath**. This path is initially somewhat overgrown, but opens out later. Follow the path towards a sand pit and there take a path to the right, avoiding the pit. Continue along the path, which soon opens out into a sandy bridleway. Keep straight to reach a junction with a sign marking the boundary of Blaxhall Heath. Now turn left and follow the track back to the car park.

POINTS OF INTEREST:

Iken Church – This classic Suffolk church is dedicated to St Botolph.

Snape Maltings – Set on the banks of the River Alde, this unique collection of 19th-century maltings includes many interesting shops and galleries. The concert hall and the Britten-Pears School for Advanced Musical Studies are home to the Aldeburgh Festival of Music and Arts as well as a year round programme of concerts and master classes.

Blaxhall Heath – Managed by Blaxhall Parish Council and Suffolk Wildlife Trust, the Heath is a section of the little remaining heathland vegetation that used to span the Suffolk coast from Lowestoft to Ipswich.

REFRESHMENTS:

None on the route, but the detour to Snape Maltings finds the Granary Tea Rooms and *Ye Old Plough and Sail Public House.*

Maps: OS Sheets Landranger 156; Pathfinder 987.

A circular walk passing Sizewell Power Station and the Sizewell Nature Reserve.

Start: At 475628, the car park on the coast near the Power Station.

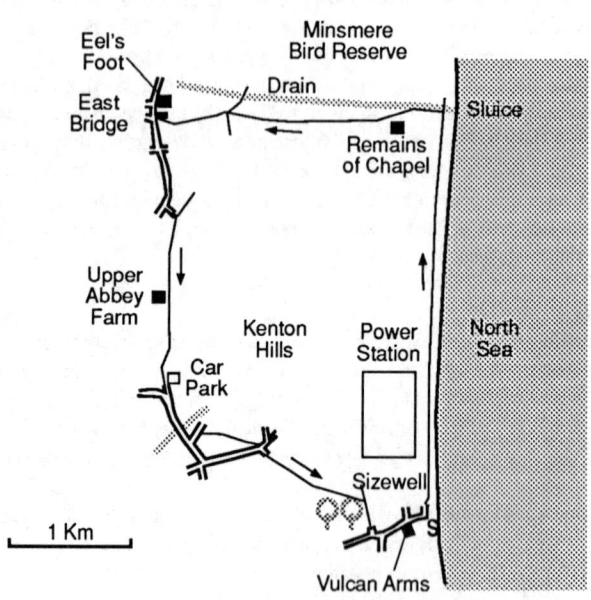

From the car park, walk on to the beach and turn left along it, heading between the **Sizewell Power Stations** and the sea. The track soon crosses a board walk and passes Sizewell A Magnox nuclear power station, on your left, and a sand dune reclamation project, on your right. The next building on your left is the new Sizewell B pressurised water reactor (PWR) nuclear power station which went 'critical' in February 1995. Next to Sizewell B is the site for the proposed third nuclear power station, Sizewell C.

Continue along the sandy track to reach Minsmere Sluice with the white Coastguard cottages in the distance. Here, turn left along a waymarked path ensuring that you are between the drainage ditches and not walking into the Minsmere Bird Reserve.

Follow the path with the main ditch on your right, passing a waymarker pointing to Eastbridge and continuing to reach a stream with a ford on your left. Cross the stream and a stile, and then follow the path across an arable field, and then pasture, on your right. Continue along the path to reach a track. Turn left and walk past Holly Cottages to reach a metalled road. For refreshments turn right here to reach the Eel's Foot public house.

To continue the walk turn left along the metalled road, passing East Bridge Farm, on the right. After another 800 yards you will reach a waymarked bridleway on the left. Take this, soon reaching a junction. Turn right and follow the bridleway past Upper Abbey Farm, on your right, and the **Kenton Hills Walks** car park, on your left.

The bridleway soon reaches the main road to Sizewell: bear left and follow the road downhill, going over a stream and then up past a waste disposal site on your left. Take the next track on the left and, after some 150 yards, cross a stile on your right, just before a cottage. Go diagonally across the field, heading towards Sizewell B in the distance. Maintain direction, crossing several stiles as you follow the path into a wood and then down the left-hand side of a house. The path then reaches a junction of tracks: turn right, and then immediately left to follow a sandy track across pasture, again heading towards Sizewell B. At a junction of tracks, turn right to reach the main road again. Turn left and follow the road past the Vulcan Arms to return to the car park.

POINTS OF INTEREST:
Kenton Hills Walks – The Hills are an area of mixed woodland crossed by four waymarked walks. Originally planted in the 1920s the woodland suffered considerable damage in the 1987 storm but has since been replanted with native hardwoods.
Sizewell Power Stations – The site has a Visitors Centre which provides an exhibition on nuclear power generation. Tours of the power stations can be provided with prior notification. Further information can be obtained by telephoning 01728-642139.

REFRESHMENTS:
The Eel's Foot, Eastbridge.
The Vulcan Arms, Sizewell.
There is also a beach cafe next to the car park.

Maps: OS Sheets Landranger 169; Pathfinder 1031.

A fine circular walk along the River Deben to Shottisham.

Start: At 309414, the car park on left-hand side of the lane leading to the Ramsholt Arms.

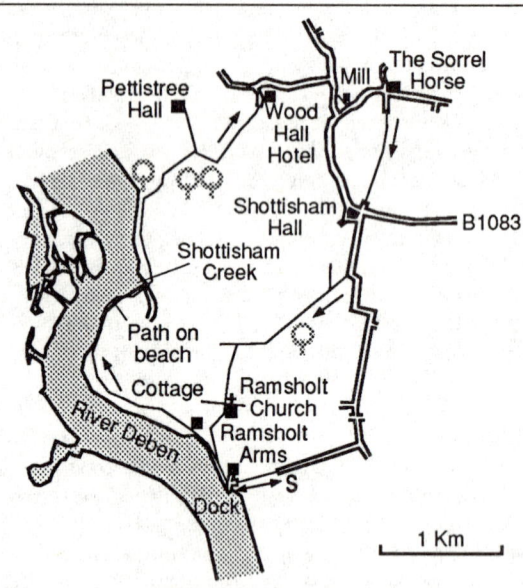

Please note that it is sometimes difficult to follow the path near Sluice Cottage during high tides.

From the car park, turn left and follow the metalled lane down to the Ramsholt Arms and the River Deben. Turn right and follow the path along the edge of the river. Just after a cottage on your right, the path goes in land but soon returns to the river's edge. Then, just before Sluice Cottage the path follows the sandy beach under the low cliff edge. Soon you reach Sluice Cottage and the Ramsholt Sluice. Continue to follow the river, but now on the landward side of the river wall. The path now becomes a green track: continue along this track, which soon turns inland, away from the river, passing a wood and some outbuildings on your left.

After a further 400 yards the track turns sharp left: turn sharp right and follow another track uphill. The track now turns sharp left, heading towards Wood Hall Hotel. Go through a metal gate and bear slightly right to reach a stile beside a wooden gate. Follow the track beyond down the left-hand side of a barn and, at its end, turn left to follow another track around to the right to reach the front of the Hotel. The track now joins a metalled lane: follow this, walking between an avenue of trees to reach a road (the B1083).

Turn right, with care, along the road, but after some 200 yards, just before the village sign for Shottisham, turn left and follow a path over a bridge and stile. Continue along the path, heading to the right of an old mill house. Continue along a driveway, going up to reach a metalled lane. Turn left and head into Shottisham village. Just past the Sorrel Horse, take a turning on the right, going up a driveway and past some cottages, on your right. Maintain direction for about a further 1000 yards to reach a road (the B1083 again). Cross, with care, and go up the lane opposite (signposted Ramsholt 2m), passing the farm buildings of Shottisham Hall on your right.

After a further 600 yards, where the road turns left, turn sharp right and follow a sandy track, with a hedgerow on your right. Soon bear left and follow the track past woods on your left. Beyond the woods the track turns right and then, just after the edge of the hedgerow on your left, turn left to follow a track heading down to **Ramsholt Church**. At the junction of tracks by the church, continue straight on, passing the church on your left. Soon the track bears right and heads down to a pasture: bear right into the pasture and then, after a few yards, bear left and head towards the corner of the field. Leave the field through a gate and climb to the river wall. Turn left to head back to the Ramsholt Arms, reversing the first few steps of the walk to return to the car park.

POINTS OF INTEREST

Ramsholt Church – In the Middle Ages Ramsholt was a settlement of some considerable size, but today the population grouped around the church is estimated to be just 34. The centre of Ramsholt is now at the dock from where a ferry service once operated across the Deben.

REFRESHMENTS:
The Ramsholt Arms, Ramsholt.
The Sorrel Horse, Shottisham.

Maps: OS Sheets Landranger 134; Pathfinder 925.
A walk around Somerleyton Hall.
Start: At 505992, the Village Pond, Lound.

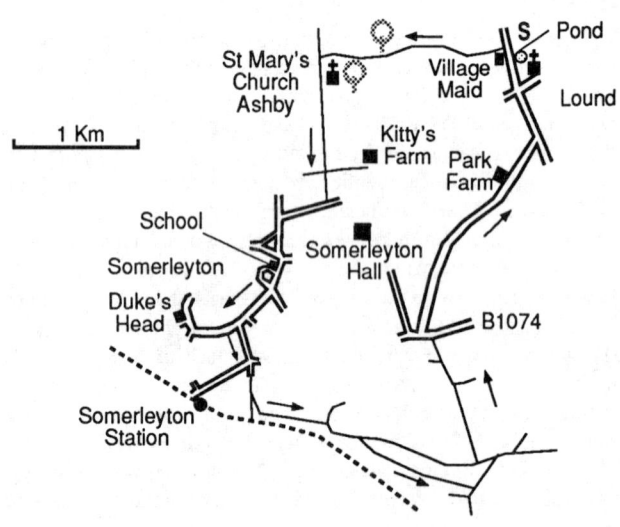

Street parking is available in Lound, but please park carefully and with consideration.

From the pond, take the bridleway to the right of the Village Maid, following it for just less than a mile, passing woodland on both your right and left. When you reach a junction of tracks, turn left to pass along the right-hand side of St Mary's Church, Ashby (i.e. walking with the church on your left). Maintain direction, passing a track on the right, to reach a crossing track. Do not turn on to this track: instead continue straight on along the left-hand side of a field, soon joining the metalled driveway of **Somerleyton Hall**.

Turn right and follow the driveway to a metalled lane. Turn left and follow the lane down to a junction. Turn left again, following the lane until it turns sharp left in front of the village school. There, keep straight on into the village of **Somerleyton**. Just past the village Post Office, on your right, turn left down Station Road. Where the road turns sharp right, continue straight on, going along a track with a farm on your left. Where the track divides, bear left and follow the track to reach a junction of tracks.

Turn right and, after a few yards, turn right again along a waymarked path. Follow this path for some $^3/_4$ mile to reach a stile and a crossing track. Turn left and follow this sandy track uphill to a T-junction. Turn left to reach, after 200 yards, a combined double and single gate on your right. Turn right here and follow the right-hand field edge. Where a track comes in from the right, continue straight on to reach a point, soon after, where your track turns sharp left. There, continue straight on along the right-hand side of a field to reach a metalled road. Turn left to reach, after a few yards, a road junction. Turn right and follow the lane for just over a mile, passing Park Farm on your left, to reach a road junction. Turn left and follow the road back into Lound to regain the start of the walk.

POINTS OF INTEREST:

Somerleyton Hall – The Hall, built in the 16th century, was the home of the Wentworth family. It was rebuilt in the 1840s to the taste of the new owner, Sir Samuel Morton Peto, the so-called "father of modern Lowestoft", a railway contractor and developer. **Somerleyton** – Somerleyton is an estate village built in the 1840/50s by Sir Samuel Morton Peto. It was considered to have far superior housing compared to other non-estate villages. Somerleyton Railway Station was built, in 1847, by the Lowestoft Harbour and Railway Company in the style of Somerleyton Hall.

REFRESHMENTS:
The Village Maid, Lound.
The Duke's Head, Somerleyton.

Walk 94   BECCLES   7m (11km)

Maps: OS Sheets Landranger 134; Pathfinder 925.
An excellent walk along the River Waveney.
Start: At 422912, the Quay car park, Beccles.

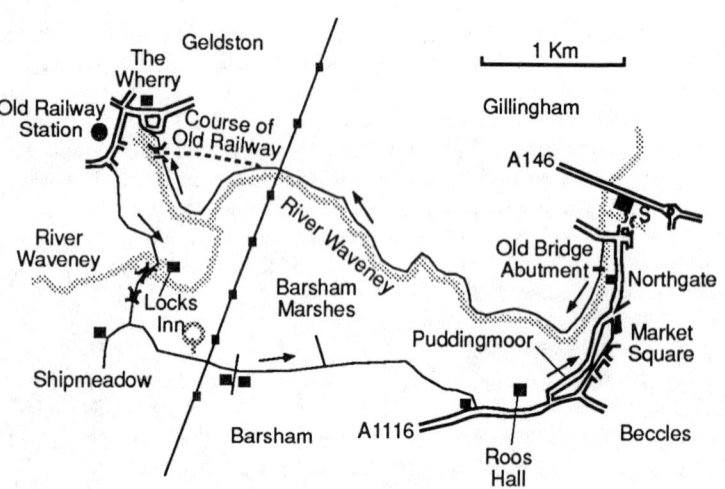

From the car park, go back to Fen Lane and, at the crossroads, turn right down Bridge Street to reach the bridge over the River Waveney. Cross the bridge and turn sharp left to go down some steps to reach the water's edge. Now walk along the riverbank, passing through the boatyard and, soon after, passing the bridge abutments of the old **Waveney Valley Railway.**

Continue on along the riverbank for some $2\frac{1}{2}$ miles to reach the Waveney's junction with the Geldeston Cut. Here, follow the bank of the Cut towards Geldeston. When you reach an old railway bridge, go under it, following the path to a driveway of Rowan Craft Marina. Turn right and follow the drive to the main road, reaching it opposite the Wherry. Turn left along the road and walk down to the crossroads. Turn left again along Station Road, passing the old Geldeston Station on your right. Continue to where the road turns right, and there turn left to follow a driveway down to the Locks Inn.

Walk to the right-hand side of the inn and go over a series of three bridges, the second bridge crossing the course of the original river. On the far side of the bridges, maintain direction, heading for the right-hand side of the field. Soon you will cross another bridge, this one over a ditch, and then head uphill to reach a stile. Cross the stile and turn left to follow a path through scrub to reach a stile and pasture. Cross the stile, turn left and head towards another stile. Cross this, and then a further stile to reach an arable field. Go along the left-hand edge of the field, soon crossing a green track. Continue along a now distinct track, passing cottages on your right. After walking for a further mile you will reach the main Beccles to Bungay road (the A1116).

Turn left and follow the road, with great care, for some 600 yards, passing **Roos Hall** on your left, to reach a lane (Puddingmoor), also on your left. Follow Puddingmoor to Market Square at the centre of **Beccles**. Now turn left and go down Northgate to regain Bridge Street and reverse the outward route along Fen Lane to return to the car park.

POINTS OF INTEREST:

Roos Hall – The Hall was built on the site of an earlier, 14th-century, manor owned by the Norman knight William De Roos. The present, 16th-century, Hall was built by Thomas Colby in the Dutch style. Colby sold the building to Sir John Suckling whose descendant, Catherine Suckling, was the mother of Horatio Nelson.

Beccles – There are many places of interest in Beccles: information on these is obtainable from the Broads Authority Tourist Office on the Quay, near the start of the walk.

Waveney Valley Railway – This line was first conceived in 1846, the Waveney Valley Railway Company being formed in 1851. However, trains did not start running to Beccles until 1863 when the company was absorbed into the Great Eastern Railway. The railways busiest time was during World War II, but thereafter traffic declined. Passenger traffic ceased in 1953 and the line finally closed in 1963.

REFRESHMENTS:

The Wherry, Geldeston.
The Locks Inn, Geldeston.
There are also numerous possibilities in Beccles.

Maps: OS Sheets Landranger 155; Pathfinder 1029.
A circular walk from the village via Edwardstone and Groton.
Start: At 963405, the White Hart, Broad Street, Boxford.

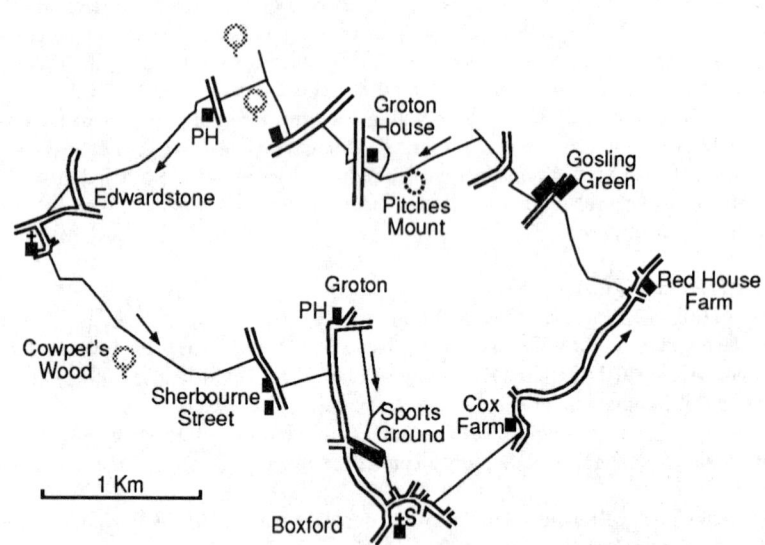

From the White Hart, turn right and follow Broad Street passing a garage, on the left, and then turn left along a path opposite River Hall. Continue along the path, crossing several fields to reach a metalled lane. Turn left and, after about 1,000 yards, turn left again along a track opposite Red House Farm. Just before the end of the track, bear left, and then right, to follow the right-hand side of the adjacent field. At the corner of the field, bear right to head towards the left-hand side of distant hedgerow, reaching a metalled lane opposite farm buildings at Gosling Green. Turn left and, just after the last house on the right, turn right to follow the right-hand edge of the field to reach a stream. Turn right, then left to cross the stream and continue to reach a metalled lane.

Cross and follow the path opposite to a wooden bridge. Turn left, cross a second bridge and follow the right-hand edge of the field beyond to reach a plantation. Turn right, then left to pass the right-hand side of Pitches Mount, the remains of a

12th-century motte and bailey castle. Continue through some conifers to reach a trackway, with a stile opposite. Cross the stile and head downhill, passing Groton House on your right, to reach some steps and a metalled lane. Cross the lane and follow the path opposite along the right-hand side of a ditch to reach another metalled lane. Turn left, and then, after some 250 yards, turn right by a pond just before a house on the right. Now follow a cross-field path, heading for the right-hand side of a wood. Follow the path along the side of the wood and, at its end, turn left to follow the path to a metalled lane. Cross the lane and take the path opposite, between bungalows. Turn left, then right to go along the right-hand side of an open field. Now maintain this general direction, soon following the course of a stream on your right, to reach a metalled lane. Cross the lane to go through the kissing gate opposite, and then bear left to head towards St Mary's Church, Edwardstone.

Go along a track on the left of the church until it turns sharp right. There, keep straight on and, just past a barn on the left, bear left to follow the left-hand side of a field to reach a large oak tree. There, bear right to go through a new plantation, and then follow a track towards a distant wood (Cowpers Wood), walking with a hedgerow on your left. Just before the wood, go over a bridge. Now walk along the left-hand side of the wood, soon crossing an open field, and then following the hedgerow on the right, heading towards distant housing. Soon, the path bears to the left: follow it across an open field to reach a metalled lane. Turn right, and then, just past Yew Tree Cottage on the left, turn left to follow a path out to another metalled lane. Turn left and head up the lane to the Fox and Hounds, **Groton**. Continue along the lane but, where it turns left, keep straight on. Just past a barn on your right, turn right and follow a trackway downhill, passing a sports ground to reach the back gardens of some houses. Turn left and follow the path behind the houses to reach the end of a driveway. Turn right and follow a path back down to Broad Street, the White Hart and the end of the walk.

POINTS OF INTEREST:

Groton – The village has many connections with the Winthrop family. John Winthrop led the great Puritan emigration to New England in 1630. He founded the city of Boston and went on to become Governor of the Massachusetts Bay Colony.

REFRESHMENTS:
The White Hart, Boxford.
The White Horse, Edwardstone.
The Fox and Hounds, Groton.

Walk 96   **FELIXSTOWE FERRY**   7m (11km)

Maps: OS Sheets Landranger 169; Pathfinder 1054.

A walk including river, coast and marshland scenery.

Start: At 329377, the car park at Felixstowe Ferry.

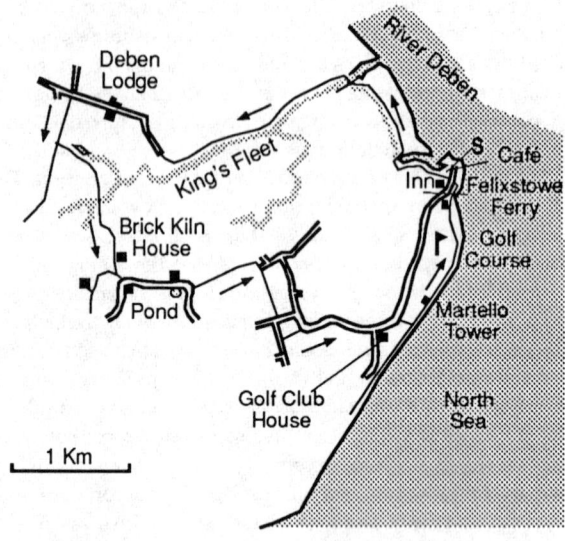

From the car park, walk back along the road to the river wall and turn right to follow the top of the wall, heading up river. (To the right across the River Deben is one of the old radar towers of **Bawdsey Manor**.)

At the end of the tarmaced section of the wall, turn right to continue along the wall, now with the saltmarsh on your right and reclaimed land on your left. Where the wall turns left, and then right, drop down to the track below and go through an iron gate. Now follow the track beside a water course (**King's Fleet**) for some 1¹/₂ miles, passing Deben Lodge on your left, to reach its junction with a lane on your right. Turn left and follow a path across an open field and down to a wooded strip. At the strip, turn left to follow a path, soon passing an old decoy pond on your left. At the end of the pond, go over the stile and bear right to head towards a waymarker at the corner of the pasture. From the waymarker, follow the right-hand edge of the field to the next corner, and then go over a bridge into the adjacent field. Turn right and follow the edge of the field to reach a trackway. Turn right and follow the track past Brick Kiln House to reach a junction of tracks. Turn left to join Gulpher Road.

Turn left and follow the road, soon passing Gulpher Pond, on your right, and Gulpher Farm, on your left. Where the road turns sharp right, take the footpath on the left, following it along the left-hand side of an open field. Just past the corner of the field you will reach a junction of paths: continue straight on to return to Gulpher Road, reaching it at a T-junction. Go straight on along Ferry Lane opposite and, just before the start of housing on your left, turn left to follow a path, soon rejoining Ferry Lane next to a pill box. Turn right along the lane to reach a T-junction opposite the golf clubhouse. Turn left and, after a few yards, turn right to follow a waymarked path across the golf course to join the sea wall. Turn left and go along the top of the sea wall, soon passing two **Martello Towers** and the Victoria public house. Continue along the wall, soon reaching the Ferry Cafe car park and the end of the walk.

POINTS OF INTEREST:

Bawdsey Manor – Built in 1886, this was the home of Sir Cuthbert Quilter until he sold it to the Air Ministry in 1936. It was here that Sir Robert Watson-Watt led the team that developed the first air defence radar warning station.

King's Fleet – It is hard to believe that this strip of water gave refuge to more than 40 ships of King Edward III's fleet in 1338 as they prepared to transport troops to France and the Battle of Crecy.

Martello Towers – The towers are two of the 75 built in 1810-12 as part of the country's defences against a Napoleonic invasion. They were copies of the Torre della Martella defensive tower in Corsica, hence the name.

REFRESHMENTS:

The Ferryboat, Felixstowe Ferry.
The Victoria, Felixstowe Ferry.
The Ferry Cafe, at the start of the walk.

Walk 97 THE RIVER DEBEN AND KIRTON CREEK   8m (13km)

Maps: OS Sheets Landranger 169; Pathfinder 1031.

A circular walk through heath, woods and salt marsh.

Start: At 273431, the car park at the Fox Inn, Newbourne.

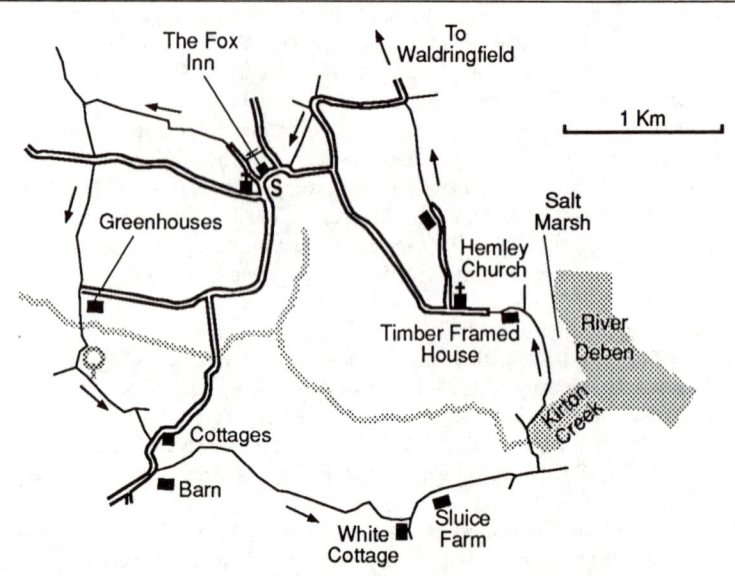

Follow the track at the left-hand side of the car park, going up a slight hill to reach an open field. The path now follows the left-hand side of the field to reach a stile – which may be hard to find – in the top left corner. Cross the stile and follow the right-hand edge of the field beyond, eventually walking between two fences up to a junction with another path. Turn left and follow the path to a metalled road. Cross the road and follow the track opposite to reach a concrete driveway. Maintain direction, passing a house on the right, heading downhill towards the bottom of the field. Cross the left-hand stile before the bottom of the hill, by the corner of some large greenhouses.

Take the path immediately on your right, following it down to a stream. Cross the stream and follow the path uphill to reach an open field. Turn left and follow a track downhill. Go over a small stream and bear left at a junction of tracks. At the top of the slope, take the path on the right, between two fences. Now follow the boundary fence on your right to reach a metalled road. Turn right along the road and, after about 200 yards, turn left along the track in front of a barn. Follow this track down to a stream and then up a sandy hill. Continue along the track, eventually passing around the right-hand side of an open field. The track eventually becomes a narrow path: continue along it to reach its junction with another, main, track. Turn left and follow this track through Sluice Farm, eventually turning left at the junction with another track to head downhill towards the River Deben.

Take the next track on the left, going down to Kirton Creek. The River Deben and Ramsholt Church are on your left. Go past the end of the Creek and then take the path on the right which follows the river's edge. Follow this riverside path over the salt marsh to reach its junction with a path going inland, on your left. Take this path, heading towards a timber-framed house. Go past the house to reach a metalled road, following it to All Saints Church, Hemley.

Turn right past the church, following the metalled road past houses, on your left, and then go along a grass track to reach the corner of another metalled road. Turn sharp left and follow the road for 200 yards. Now, where the road bends sharp left, follow it to reach a junction with a path and bridleway on your right. Follow the path – go straight on – crossing a field towards a gap between distant trees. At the far edge of the field, follow the hedge on your left for 20 yards, then turn sharp left to follow a path – which may be overgrown – to the edge of woodland. Follow the path down a steep bank to reach a road and turn right. After 50 yards, turn right at a road junction and then left into **Newbourne Springs Nature Reserve**.

Take the path in the top right-hand corner of the car park, following it beside a stream. At its T-junction with another waymarked path, turn left, walking through the reed beds, to reach a stile and a junction with a track. Turn left and follow this track back to the car park.

POINTS OF INTEREST:

Newbourne Springs Nature Reserve – The Reserve is owned by Anglian Water and supplied the drinking water for Felixstowe from the early 1930s until the early 1980s. It is now managed for wildlife conservation by the Suffolk Wildlife Trust. Inside the reserve you can still see the old pump house – now the Visitors Centre – and the original water gauge.

REFRESHMENTS:

The Fox Inn, Newbourne.

Walk 98　　Otley and Helmingham　　$8\frac{1}{2}$m ($13\frac{1}{2}$km)

Maps: OS Sheets Landranger 156; Pathfinder 1008.

A circular walk from Otley to Helmingham.

Start: At 205549, St Mary's Church, Otley.

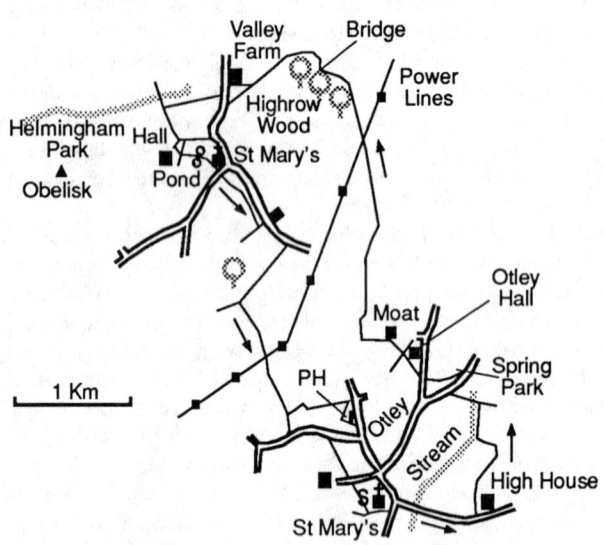

From St Mary's Church, go down the lane opposite and, just before reaching High House, on your left, turn left to go along a bridleway. Go through a wooden gate, cross a plantation to its far left-hand corner and then go into the adjacent field on the left. Bear right and head for the far right-hand corner of the field. There, turn right and follow the edge of the field to its end, and then turn left to follow a now-distinctive bridleway out to a metalled lane. Turn right and, after a few yards, turn left into Spring Park. At the end of this close, pass between houses and follow a path to reach another lane. Cross the lane and follow the footpath opposite, going to the left of **Otley Hall.**

Follow the path to a green lane. Cross this and follow the cross-field path opposite to reach the edge of a wooded moat. Turn left and, after a few yards, turn right along the right-hand edge of a field to reach an open area. Bear right, then left to follow a path for some 500 yards to reach a T-junction of paths next to a drainage ditch. Continue straight on here, following a cross-field path to reach the hedgerow opposite. Bear left and follow the edge of several fields, going under the electricity pylons, to reach Highrow Wood. Turn right and, after a few yards, turn left to go along the side of the wood. Soon you will reach a bridge on your right: turn right and cross a small pasture to its left-hand corner. Go through a hedge and turn left. At the end of this field, follow a track for some 600 yards and, where it turns sharp right, keep straight on to reach a bridge, crossing this to reach a metalled lane. Turn right, and then left to follow a path into Helmingham Park. Once you are in the park, follow the stream on your right to reach a bridge, on your right. Turn left here and head towards the front of **Helmingham Hall**.

Once past the Hall, maintain direction, soon going over a bridge across a pond and continuing to reach a road in front of St Mary's Church. Cross the road and follow the footpath opposite down to the Otley road. Continue along the edge of the field, walking parallel to the road to reach a bridge at a junction of paths opposite a cottage. Now continue along the road for some 150 yards to reach a pair of wooden gates on the right. Turn right here along a path which may not be waymarked. Follow the right-hand side of a field up to woodland and, when you come to the second field boundary on the left, turn left and follow the right-hand edge of the field towards the distant pylons. Maintain direction along several field edges to reach a metalled lane. Turn left and, after a few yards, turn right along a waymarked path. Just after a bridge in the corner of the field, turn left and go along a path to reach a farm track. Cross the track and, after a few yards, turn left through some scrub to head back to St Mary's Church and the end of the walk.

POINTS OF INTEREST:

Otley Hall – This 15th-century house, surrounded by a moat, was built by Robert Gosnold. The Gosnold family's rise to manorial lordship came about in the 15th century but unfortunately, being Royalists, they never recovered from the punishments and financial penalties incurred after the Civil War.

Helmingham Hall – The Hall is the home of the Tollymache family who acquired it in the 15th century. Today the family is known for the activities of Douglas Tollemache, co-founder the Tolly Cobbold brewery.

REFRESHMENTS:
The White Hart, Otley.

Walk 99   MINSMERE BIRD RESERVE   9m (14$\frac{1}{2}$km)

Maps: OS Sheets Landranger 156; Pathfinder 966.

A walk around Minsmere Bird Reserve.

Start: At 479707, the beach car park at Dunwich.

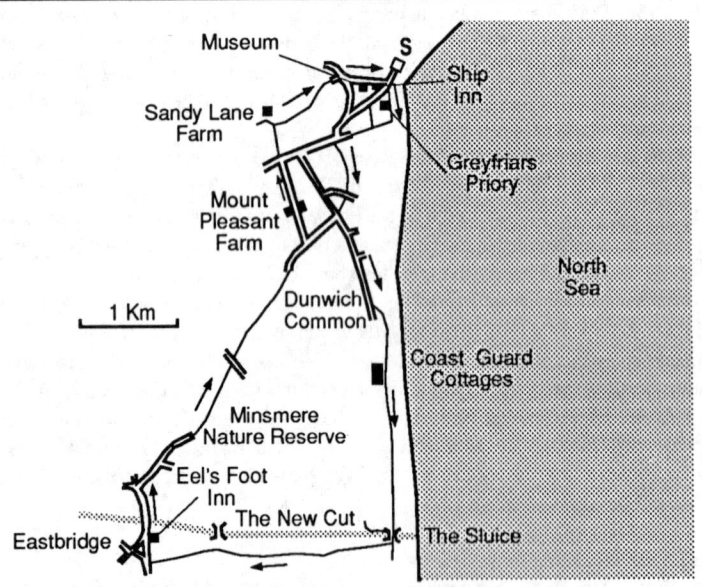

Leave the car park via the car exit and walk back to the Ship Inn. Go to the left of the inn, then take the waymarked path on the left, following it past Greyfriars Priory and heading along the cliff top. After a while the path joins a track coming from the cliff edge: turn right and follow the track under a footbridge, continuing along it to reach a road. Bear left along the road, but after a few yards turn left along a waymarked track, following it through woodland and continuing to reach a small lane. Turn left along the lane to reach the outskirts of the **Minsmere Bird Reserve**.

Just past a hut on the left, take the path to the cliff top, following the cliff towards the coastguard cottages. Go to the left of the cottages, down steps and follow the track towards Sizewell. Soon you will come to a bridge (The Sluice). Cross this to reach a footpath on the right. Follow this waymarked path along the south side of the drainage ditch (The New Cut) to reach the road at Eastbridge. Turn right along the road, passing the Eel's Foot Inn on the right. Continue along the road, eventually turning right towards the Bird Reserve. Where the road bears right to the Visitors Centre, continue straight on along a bridleway through woodland. Follow the bridleway past open ground, eventually crossing a small lane leading to the Reserve. Continue through the woods to reach a junction, with paths on your right and left. Take the path on the left, going past Mount Pleasant Farm and continuing to a road.

Cross and follow a track to Sandy Lane Farm. In front of the farm, turn right along another track, following it to a road junction by St James Church. Now take the road opposite, passing the church on your right. Continue past the **Dunwich Museum** and the Ship Inn, turning left to return to the car park.

POINTS OF INTEREST:

Dunwich Heath and Minsmere Bird Reserve – Dunwich Heath is owned by the National Trust and consists of 214 acres of natural heathland and beach. It lies beside the RSPB's Minsmere Bird Reserve, the whole area being a delight for naturalists and ornithologists.

Dunwich Museum – Once an important Roman town and port, most of Dunwich now lies under the sea having suffered from coastal erosion for centuries. The museum is a must for anyone interested in the history of the town and its demise.

REFRESHMENTS:

The Ship Inn, Dunwich.

The Eel's Foot Inn, Eastbridge.

From March to November meals are also available at the Flora Tea Rooms on the beach at Dunwich. Opening times can be confirmed by telephoning 01728 648687.

Maps: OS Sheets Landranger 144; Pathfinder 962.

A long easy walk through forest and across heathland.

Start: At 788715, the Rampart Field Picnic Site car park, Icklingham.

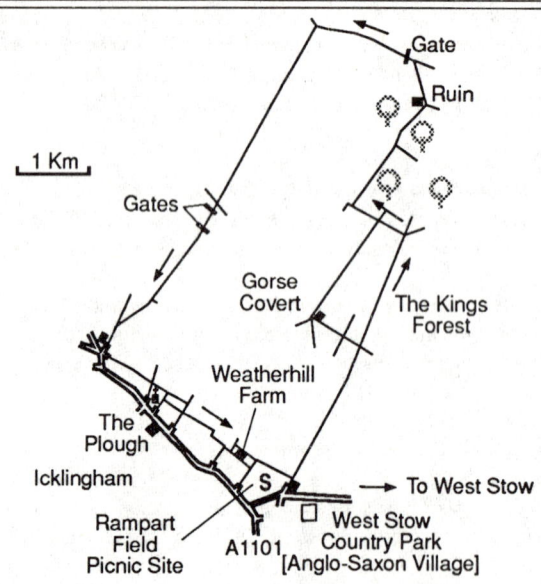

From the car park, near the **West Stow Country Park**, cut across the heath to reach the minor road to West Stow. Turn left and follow the road for a few yards to reach a track on the left just before a cottage. This track is the Icknield Way. Turn left and follow the Way through the forest, maintaining direction at all times. After just over two miles the track goes slightly uphill and reaches a track, on your left, numbered 208. Reaching this point will take about an hour from the road.

Turn left down the track to reach a junction of tracks. Continue straight on, soon reaching the edge of the forest. Turn right and walk for about 1 mile to reach a ruined building. There, bear slightly left and follow the main track out of the forest. Just beyond a metal-bar gate, turn left along a metalled track, soon going through a wooden gate. Continue along this metalled track for about $^3/_4$ mile to reach a junction of tracks.

Turn left and follow a track for some $1^1/_2$ miles to where it turns to the right. Now continue straight on to reach a gate. Go through and follow the track beyond to reach a second gate. Go through this gate and continue straight on for a further mile to meet a track coming in from the right, just before some cottages, also on the right. Just beyond the cottages, take a trackway on the left, following it behind the houses in Icklingham. Where you meet a cross-track, continue straight on until you reach a track on your right. Now turn right and follow the track for some 100 yards.

For refreshments, continue straight on along the track, passing All Saints Church on your right. At the main road, the A1101, turn left, with care, to reach the Plough, on the opposite side of the road.

To continue the route, turn left along a track, with wire fencing to both the left and right, following it to reach a stile. Go over and walk along the right-hand side of an arable field. At the end of the field, go over a stile, turn right and then left to follow the left-hand side of an arable field. Soon you will reach a track leading to Weatherhill Farm. Follow this, but just before the farm take a path on the left. After a few yards, turn right and go along the right-hand side of a field. Follow the field edge to reach a track, then continue straight on, soon reaching a junction with the Icknield Way. Turn right and follow the track to a metalled lane. Turn right and follow the lane back to the car park.

POINTS OF INTEREST:
West Stow Country Park – The park contains a reconstructed Anglo-Saxon village on a site that is known to have been occupied 1500 years ago.

REFRESHMENTS:
The Plough, Icklingham.